LATINA LEADERSHIP LESSONS

FIFTY LATINAS SPEAK

Edited by
Delia García

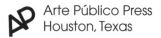
Arte Público Press
Houston, Texas

Latina Leadership Lessons: Fifty Latinas Speak is published in part with support from the National Endowment for the Arts and the Alice Kleberg Reynolds Foundation. We are grateful for their support.

Recovering the past, creating the future

Arte Público Press
University of Houston
4902 Gulf Fwy, Bldg 19, Rm 100
Houston, Texas 77204-2004

Cover design by Mora Design

Cataloging-in-Publication (CIP) Data is available.

22 23 24   4 3 2 1

CONTENTS

DEDICATION

I dedicate this book to all the women who shaped me, especially my three grandmothers, mother, sisters, nieces, goddaughters, Kappa Delta Chi Latina Service Sorority sisters, National Hispana Leadership Institute (NHLI) leonas and extended *familia,* especially those who were a part of my journey in writing this book. I dedicate this book to the women who have paved the way and I stand on their shoulders, and to our rising leaders who will create more ways using some of these lessons and sharing their own wisdom to make this world a compassionate place for those we love. My ancestors sacrificed their lives to make it possible for my sisters and me to have the life we have. I know it is my responsibility to do the same, using my God-given gifts for a purpose greater than myself, with God showing me how to take who I am and who I want to be and do for others what many have done for me, *con puro amor,* with pure love.

A special thank you to the women who opened their arms and homes to allow me to write this book, including my mother Carmen Rosales, sorority sister Sandra Chacón, cousin Diana Maldonado, NHLI sister Patricia Mejía and hermanas Teresa Nino and Lucero Ortiz. *Muchísimas gracias* to Rev. Andy Hernández, Dr. Ellen Clark, Sandra Cisneros, Angela Cervantes and Anel Flores for your advice and guidance on writing this book.

Photo by Heather Hazzan

FOREWORD BY DOLORES HUERTA

Who is a Latina leader and what lessons can she share with us? In *Latina Leadership Lessons: Fifty Latinas Speak,* three generations of Latina leaders from twenty-four states and different corners of our country share their leadership lessons and wisdom. I have personally been with many of these women in various leadership gatherings and witnessed them fighting to protect our rights, our bodies and our freedoms.

Latina leaders have had to overcome racial discrimination and gender bias and have often been told by society and persons close to them that the roles they aspired to were "not for them," that they were "not qualified." They sought dreams that seemed illusive, opportunities that had to be discerned and discovered, goals that were too distant to perceive. In spite of all the barriers, they surpassed, survived and overcame disappointments and hurdles. They made sacrifices to reach their leadership positions. Now, these Latina leaders enact policies and implement programs to serve their communities and the public.

When we see the various obstacles they met on their path to leadership, it will help us to avoid, or copy, whichever style fits the need in our own personal paths as we acquire our own leadership skills. We can learn from their experiences to avoid the pitfalls that they encountered, thus making our journey less arduous and difficult.

First: Latina leaders set a unique standard for "true women's leadership." The leadership lessons in this book are empowering; our women leaders show us not to hold ourselves back, to erase our self-doubts, to be courageous. These lessons will hopefully inspire more women to ascend to leadership.

Second: Latina leaders are hardly recognized. Women's accomplishments are often overlooked. Thankfully, I had and have women in my life who have inspired my own leadership. They include women of all ages and backgrounds. My mother Alicia St. John Chávez was my first example of leadership. Others include my Girl Scout leader and feminists Gloria Steinman, Hilda L. Solis, Eleanor Smeal, Hillary Clinton and the author of this book, Delia García.

This book was written for various audiences. However, this book is for the Latina who wants to be seen and heard, while she connects to each word about herself. Ultimately, a Latina leader embodies servant leadership. By reading and applying the lessons learned in this book, you will increase your ability to develop and enhance your own leadership skills and pass them on to others. The young leaders I meet today are so inspiring. They are the change champions on the front lines and will accomplish more than we can ever imagine. As a leader, you will attain the ability to craft a culture that supports transformative leadership.

Moreover, we learn how to own our power from our sister leaders in this book. When we act in service and gratitude, we impact our world more than we could have ever imagined. When we witness our impact, the world becomes more beautiful, especially for those we love. Women's leadership is desperately needed in our world today. Women are the hope for the future. I trust and know the women in this book will make this happen, especially the author and my dear sister, Delia García. *¡Adelante y sí se puede!*

INTRODUCTION

I compiled *Latina Leadership Lessons: Fifty Latinas Speak* to support our transformation into the leaders we must be, the leaders our country desperately needs now and in the future. Let us ask ourselves, "What was the purpose I was put on this Earth for?" If we do not know, then we need to listen and pay attention to the signs in front of us. If we are breathing on this Earth, we have a purpose. It is imperative to believe in and embrace our life purpose, and it is never too late to do so.

Let us wrap our arms around each other in a virtual or in-person loving embrace. This book attempts to do that in the sense of sharing lessons we learned to empower us to be the leaders we wish to have running our world. The women in this book are excellent examples of outstanding leaders who are like you and me. We can choose to learn from their lessons, or not. You do not have to be Latina in order to learn from these powerful lessons. We may see there are similarities with other groups of women; we may share many of the same challenges. There is also a learning opportunity for men to learn more about women leaders, and to share these lessons with their daughters, wives, sisters, nieces, aunts and all extended family.

Leadership development is an engaging activity. When we think of leadership, we think representation matters, people matter and you matter. For example, seeing a reflection of myself in leaders inspired me to imagine possibilities for myself and for my community. Also, not seeing a reflection of myself in leaders inspired me to do something about that. One of my favorite prayers is the Serenity Prayer: "God grant me the serenity to accept the things I cannot change, the courage to change the things I can, and the wisdom to know the difference." This made me realize I could write a book that would provide the lessons learned by powerful leaders in our United States. *Latina Leadership Lessons* reflects what America looks like and will grow to look like, including you and me. It is my goal that this book serve as a symbol of what leadership looks like and can be, coupled with new ways to create more leadership guidance.

It is said that to empower a woman is to empower a community. *Latina Leadership Lessons* can empower us, no matter what stage of life we are in. In fact, words can empower us and others. This book intentionally uses words to empower us through real life examples. But first, it is important for us to acknowledge some of the challenges that women face. Sometimes, we have a tendency to be self-deprecating, dismissive of praise and overly polite when asking for something or giving instruction, possibly for fear of what others might think or out of a desire for their validation. I admit I have been, and try to discontinue to be, a user of filler words that include *just, sort of, umm* . . . which makes a speaker appear less confident and insecure. We must not be apologetic for having an opinion or daring to exist. Nor should we apologize too much or for the wrong things, because that is not the example of what we would want for our daughters or nieces to do or see. It is a good thing to examine one's own behavior and practices, and to invite constructive criticism, but not to expect it all the time.

Like many of us, I am guilty of the imposter syndrome, where I have and still sometimes question my own abilities. This is so wrong on so many levels, because I know I am a *chingona,* a strong woman leader—like author Sandra Cisneros, I am even reclaiming that word in the process.

It is tough being a woman leader, and even tougher being a leader as a woman of color. The powerful truth is we are used to working harder, and studies show that we are natural collaborators and listeners. On the other hand, studies also show women leaders are more challenged to communicate effectively about our own needs and goals. We know that practice makes *almost* perfect, so learning more ways to practice is important.

Leaders are continually learning ways to serve better. There are even some not-so-hard actions to begin practicing. A Washington University study states that a quick way to be more assertive immediately is to stand up. Standing up can automatically make you assertive, including walking and simply moving around. It also inspires creative thinking and collaboration. We can adopt body language, facial expressions, voice tone and gestures to demonstrate confidence and assertiveness. We shall stand tall (even if we are 5 feet tall), shoulders back, chin up, and adopt a power pose—hands on our hips—like our *abuelitas* taught us when we witnessed their fierceness. We can also stand feet apart with our hands folded together as if holding a baseball.

The face of our country is changing; it is now looking more diverse. For this reason, it is crucial we have leaders who look, think and act like us. At this moment in American history, there are many opportunities for us to participate in the ongoing process of making our nation. President Joe Biden appointed one Latina as a cabinet secretary in his administration, Isabella Casi-llas Guzmán, administrator of the US Small Business Administration; he also appointed other Latinas to key positions. These choices are a good start, and we expect to see this continue to be the case in future administrations. Meanwhile, it is imperative we prepare ourselves for those opportunities in government and elsewhere. We can leverage our growing energized voices to ensure representation on all levels of business, government, philanthropy, education and every other sector. Our country's communities of color are always impacted disproportionately, and we must be at the table addressing the needed change to equitable policies in the years ahead. If we are not at the table, we will be on the menu. We must recreate our world, woman-by-woman, Latina-by-Latina, as it is ours to discover and recreate among others.

Women serve disproportionately in essential industries, including hospitality, travel, agriculture and domestic. This makes women of color vulnerable. They often serve as caregivers, cleaners and perform menial labor while also being mothers and heads of household. Women can be leaders in reforming occupational industries but they must be at the table to offer solutions they know personally would work. Small business owners, the majority of whom are women, lack access to credit and other support offered to large firms. For instance, Deferred Action for Childhood Arrivals (DACA) students did not have access to student aid relief. Women, especially Latinas also should have a seat at the table when discussing the development of policies for DACA and other plans that impact our families and friends. We need to make our voices heard about the insecurity of housing, food, domestic work and access to unemployment benefits.

Our country has witnessed families ripped apart at our southern border, and still many have not been reunited with their children. We continue to witness racial injustices on television, in our workplaces, in our neighborhoods and within the criminal justice systems. All of it impacts us, but quite often we are not at the table to make decisions that will confront and correct these injustices. When we do engage, bringing along our personal experiences, better informed policies are made.

It is important to acknowledge that the US Census indicates that Latinas mainly make up a young population. Latinas are also first-to-third generation US residents, and they are part of the 51% female population that makes up 47% of the national work force. According to the Census, women are the fastest growing group of entrepreneurs, and Latina women are at the forefront. Leadership Research Institute studies show that the increasing number of female leaders brings more success and profitability, acknowledging that leadership is about ability and not gender.

We are experiencing a transformation of the United States in the twenty-first century and there is a sense of urgency for fresh, new leadership. I chose to write about leadership because this is an area where we women naturally shine. Women have natural leadership abilities, including but not limited to collaboration, communication, compassion and active listening. Women leaders can be intrinsic to success. Women possess a blend of management styles, which make businesses stronger. Women inherently lead groups and organizations just as we do at home as mothers or as siblings in a large family. Women lead businesses, nations, households, public organizations, against incredible odds.

Only over the last one hundred years, more opportunities have opened up for women. Yet, double standards still exist. For example, to openly show emotion hurts women, yet it helps men in politics. However, women excel at transformational leadership by remaining to be assertive and demonstrating compassion and strong communication skills as natural strengths. Women continue to move forward, regardless of whether we receive accolades or not. Although there seems to be a shift to embrace women leaders, there are solid barriers for women of color. Women of color struggle to be heard as we continue to not be at the decision-making tables. This is where we as leaders can come in and flex our leadership muscle. We have solid solutions to offer from firsthand knowledge. Today, there is greater opportunity to be at the decision-making table, and we can create more ways for other women of color to join.

Latina Leadership Lessons is an attempt to share some of the best ways to live as a leader. Fifty Latina leaders across the United States share their best practices on how they became more powerful and created additional networks of leaders. Now the focus is on you, as you are the most important person, reading this right now. You, we, have what it takes to be a leader, and extraordinary leaders take the responsibility seriously to develop and create more leaders, all while falling in love with the process of becoming the best version of ourselves. The fact of the matter is we leaders can all contribute something to make this world a better place for our families and friends. We each have different strengths, but when we use our strengths combined with our passion and joy, we will absolutely create a better world. When our personal identities become fully aligned to serve, we will experience our authentic power and purpose in life.

In compiling these lessons from this phenomenal group of Latina leaders (a national snapshot), I wanted to offer examples of real leaders and what is possible for us to achieve. Additionally, in these fifty Latina leaders, we can see there is a cultural concept to leadership. The lens in which we view leadership is influenced by our lived experiences. Primarily, these leaders operate from a unity group perspective instead of as individuals; they demonstrate transformative leadership that activates inclusivity as much as possible. There is a unique aspect to Latina leadership that is important to note: there is leadership among our undocumented women leaders. An example is a DACA student who looks over her shoulder every day and carries an immense amount of anxiety of her family possibly being ripped apart, but she nevertheless works and attends school. Another example is the DREAMer mother who organizes other mothers to fight for the children they brought to the United States to give them a better life while risking their own life and freedom in the process. This is a different type of courage and leadership. We own these powerful stories, but sometimes feel the need to keep this truth and ourselves in the shadows.

Our lessons begin with one of the United States' treasured civil rights leaders, one of my dear mentors, Dolores Huerta. She has demonstrated leadership for decades and continues to do so into her 90s. She has organized and led groups for human rights and social justice over the decades, during which time she was arrested twenty-two times for participating in non-violent civil disobedience activities and strikes. She literally took a beating from a San Francisco police officer in 1988 during a peaceful protest; the baton-beating caused significant internal bleeding, broken ribs and the removal of her spleen in emergency surgery. She has often encountered criticism based on both gender and ethnic stereotypes. She had started her career as a teacher, but then decided that she could do more for the hungry and barely clothed farmworkers' children in her classrooms by helping their parents win more equitable working conditions. In the late 1950s she worked with César Chávez to organize farmworkers. In 1962, they co-founded the National Farm Workers Association, before it was the United Farm Workers. They organized the Delano grape strike in 1965 in California, and she was the lead negotiator in the worker's contract that was created after the strike. She is the originator of the phrase, "*Sí se puede*," which has become a widespread anthem among civil rights activists and even politicians. We all stand on her shoulders.

In expanding our view of leadership, it is imperative to recognize the young leaders who are impacting real change for our communities. There are five powerful examples in this book, including Claudia Flores of Washington, DC, Hareth Andrade of Virginia, Lorena Tule-Romain of Texas, Barbara Gomez-Aguiñaga of Nebraska and María Gabriela "Gaby" Pacheco of Florida, who walked 1,500 miles from Miami to the White House in Washington, DC to advocate for a pathway to citizenship for immigrant youth. When I served as the Executive Director for the National Migrant and Seasonal Head Start Association in Washington, DC, I had the distinct honor to work with DREAMer mothers and farmworker families, including Karelia Harding of Oregon and interns: Eva Alvarez of Washington, who is now serving as a public policy coordinator in Michigan, and Yesenia Calderon of Florida, who is serving as an immigration attorney.

In the world of business, Latinas are forces to be reckoned with as entrepreneurs and owners of restaurants, hotels, public relations firms and heads of chambers of commerce. They represent the fastest growing group of entrepreneurs per capita. Corporate leaders in this book include Lidia S. Martínez of California and Yolanda Camarena of Kansas and former chamber of commerce executive Diana Maldonado of Texas. Other business leaders are Angelique Sina of Virginia, María Robles Meier of New Mexico, Laura Barberena of Texas and my mother Carmen Rosales of Kansas.

In foreign affairs, Latinas are a growing presence with more representation. Included in this book are Ambassador Carmen Cantor of Virginia and Helga Flores Trejo of Washington, DC. Latinas who were elected to the local, state and federal levels, include Congresswoman Sylvia Garcia of Texas, former Illinois State Representative Maria Antonia "Toni" Berrios, former Indiana State Representative Mara Candelaria Reardon, former Colorado State House Speaker Crisanta Duran, Palm Springs City Councilwoman Grace Garner, Virginia State Delegate Elizabeth Guzmán, Hawaii State Senator Michelle N. Kidani, former Texas State Representative Diana Maldonado, former California Assemblywoman and Los Angeles Board Supervisor Gloria Molina, New Jersey State Assemblywoman Annette Quijano, former Virgin Islands State Senator Nereida "Nellie" Rivera-O'Reilly, Utah State Senator Luz Escamilla, Los Angeles Board Supervisor and former US Secretary of Labor and California Congresswoman Hilda L. Solis, former San Juan Mayor Carmen Yulín Cruz Soto, Arizona State Commissioner Anna Tovar, former Texas State Senator Leticia Van de Putte, former Miami Commissioner Luz Urbáez Weinberg and Harris County Judge Lina Hidalgo.

Among the other fields represented are Attorney Maria Lucero Ortiz of Washington, DC; scientists Frances Colón of Florida and broadband leader Roxana Barboza of California; religious leaders Reverend Zanté García of Texas; military leaders

Ingrid Durán and Letitia "Leti" Gómez of Washington, DC; and non-profit organization and foundation leaders Sindy M. Benavides of Virginia, Helen Iris Torres of California and Patricia Mejia of Texas. Latina transgender leaders include Joanna Cifredo of Puerto Rico and Frankie Gonzales-Wolfe of Texas. The health care leaders Annabel Mancillas of Kansas and Dr. Ann-Gel S. Palermo of New York. And, lastly, leaders in journalism and writing include Dr. Victoria M. DeFrancesco Soto of Akansas, Lupita Colmenero of Texas and Angela Cervantes of Kansas.

EVA ALVAREZ

Eva Alvarez was born on December 24, 1992, in Othello, Washington. She is the proud daughter of immigrant parents from Mexico who fed America as migrant workers picking apples and cherries, along with their seven children. She earned her Master in Public Administration (nonprofit management and leadership) from Western Michigan University in 2020. She earned her bachelor's degree in Political Science with a minor in Criminal Justice from Washington State University in 2011. Alvarez has served as the Michigan Immigrant Rights Center Public Policy Coordinator since April 2019. Prior to this, she served as the US Department of Justice Accredited Representative and Outreach Advocate for the Michigan Immigrant Rights Center (2017-2019). Before that, she was an Outreach Advocate at the Farmworker Legal Services (2016-2017). Alvarez focuses on advocating for and influencing local, state and federal policy formation impacting immigrants. She works to ensure that policies are a true reflection of the country's values by being inclusive of immigrants and their families. She has also represented clients before the Executive Office of Immigration Review and the Department of Homeland Security. She helped launch Empowering Latina Leaders and Advocates for Success, the first professional network in Southwest Michigan with the mission to enrich and elevate Latina leaders and allies to become bridge builders and change agents in southwest Michigan. In 2019, Eva received the Western Michigan University School of Public Administration Emerging Scholar Award, and in 2018 she was awarded the Vision Award by the Hispanic Latino Commission of Michigan. The Vision Award recognizes an individual serving as a role model and advocate for the Hispanic/Latinx Community who has demonstrated leadership and creativity that makes them an inspiration to others. She has served as an advisory board member for the Migrant Labor Housing Advisory since 2020 with the Michigan Department of Agriculture and Rural Development and the Kalamazoo County Identification Program with the Kalamazoo County government since 2019.

cᴓ᥆ ᥆ᴕ

Eva's Top 10 Leadership Lessons

1. **Be a leader, then lead.** Your priority as a leader should be to lead yourself well before you lead others. I find it important to understand your leadership style.
2. **Establish your personal mission.** Align passion with purpose. Defining your personal mission will help you stay focused. Why do you do what you do?
3. **Always pay it forward.** We did not get to where we are alone. Someone paved the way for us. Help pave the way for others.
4. **You are the master of your fate.** You have no one to blame but yourself. You hold the wheel. You decide your destination, not others.
5. **Become a bridge builder.** Build relationships with people who agree and disagree with you. We need to build more bridges with each other and create less division.
6. **Never forget where you come from.** Stay true to yourself wherever you go and never forget who and what has brought you to where you are.
7. **Listen, listen, listen.** It is not always about you. Listen to what others have to say and listen to respond. Do not listen just to listen.
8. **Practice what you preach.** Walk the talk. Do not have discrepancies between what you say you want to do and what you do. It will affect your credibility to yourself and others.
9. **Evolve continously.** People and work styles are always changing, and you should too. Always be two steps ahead of the game.
10. **Do not allow others to define you.** It is okay if the doors close on you multiple times; this does not define who you are, what you have to offer or your potential. You, better than anyone else, know your potential.

HARETH ANDRADE-AYALA

Hareth Andrade-Ayala was born in June 1993 in La Paz, Bolivia and is a first-generation immigrant. She came to the United States in 2001 and is a Deferred Action for Childhood Arrivals (DACA) recipient. In 2015, she graduated with a bachelor's in International Relations at Trinity Washington University. She has been serving as a DREAM activist in Virginia since 2011 and was a member of the Bridge Project Team (2014-2015), where she engaged both political parties around immigration reform issues. The DREAMers of Virginia won domicile status for undocumented youth with DACA, with Andrade-Ayala serving as a lead advocate, expanding the eligibility for in-state tuition in the Commonwealth. In 2016, she served on the Democratic National Convention Credentials Committee. A year later, she served as the political director for the Ralph Northam for Virginia governor campaign and in 2019 as the deputy field director for the Virginia Senate Majority Leader Dick Saslaw. Andrade-Ayala has organized national campaigns for immigrant rights and helped with rallies around the issue of deportations. As a DACA actress, she starred in Jhon Daversa's Grammy award-winning album, *American Dreamers* and in the Grammy-nominated music video, *Wake Me Up*, by Aloe Blacc. She has won awards as a vocalist, including Best Large Jazz Ensemble Album at the 61st Grammy Awards in 2018 and the We Are Emily Award in 2016. She was also awarded the Mexican American Legal Defense & Education Fund DREAM Activist Award in 2012. She is a graduate student at the Catholic University of America in Washington, DC. Andrade-Ayala works at Mi Familia Vota on increasing civic engagement in Latino communities nationwide.

ℰℒ) ⏀ℒ

Hareth's Top 10 Leadership Lessons

1. **A little help from self-awareness:** Learning to look at myself from the outside in has helped me become a more intentional leader and to contextualize situations that require critical decision-making.
2. **It's okay to feel scared:** Feeling scared is something I have learned to be okay with. This has helped me go the extra mile to live some of my dreams in real life.
3. **Taking care of yourself is not selfish:** When I feel overwhelmed with responsibilities, I remind myself that nothing is more important than taking care of myself. It takes practice and humility to really let go of everything and just rest.
4. **Lock in some habits:** Reading has sparked a kind of curiosity that has opened my mind. I've found different patterns of language and ideas to help me communicate more genuinely with the community.
5. **Take a stand:** It's okay to take a strong stand; leading is born from sharing your most vulnerable experiences and opinions with others.
6. **Ask questions:** I've learned to let go of feeling a little uncomfortable and started approaching people I admire with professional questions. I learned that most people would love to tell you more about themselves, and now those people are some of my strongest supporters, mentors and friends.
7. **Volunteer:** If you're wondering where to begin, this is how I started my journey and how I got to meet others in the movement. Helpfulness is never forgotten.
8. **Millennials are unique leaders:** We are next in line to inherit and tackle some of the most important world issues. Use your platform to create leadership opportunities for others. It will take all of us to make a difference.

9. **Manage your time:** Your time is valuable, and your work is worth it. Spend more time doing what you know you are good at.
10. **Immigrant millennials are rocking it:** Be proud of your story, culture and background. Your tenacity to overcome all of the obstacles in front of you is beautiful and human. You are not alone.

LAURA BARBERENA

Laura Barberena was born on January 4, 1967, in Austin, Texas, and has dual citizenship with the United States of America and Mexico. Her father was born and raised in Mexico, immigrated to the United States and became an American citizen after marrying her mother and serving in the National Guard. Her mother is a Mexican American, born in the United States. She earned her B.S. in Radio, Television and Film from the University of Texas at Austin in 1990 and her Master of Arts in International Relations from St. Mary's University in San Antonio in 2003. Barberena earned her doctorate in Political Communications Language at the University of Texas at Austin in 2016. Barberena is the president and owner of VIVA Politics, LLC, located in San Antonio, Texas. Her firm specializes in political communications and civic engagement and manages political campaigns, including producing political direct mail, radio spots, television commercials and other campaign materials. Barberena also produces social media campaigns in English and Spanish, prepares organizational strategic plans, conducts candidate trainings and designs and implements qualitative and quantitative research projects. Barberena co-authored a manual for the Democratic National Committee titled *The Latino Campaign Guide: a Manual for Reaching Hispanic American Voters*. Barberena is a faculty member for the Latino Academy, a campaign school for the Southwest Voter Registration and Education Project. As a consultant to the National Democratic Institute, Barberena traveled to the Dominican Republic, where she conducted training classes for more than eighty participants interested in running for political office. In November 2017, Barberena and Delia García launched The Lista Project, a comprehensive leadership training program focused on Latina women living in the United States who are interested in running for elected office.

ᥱᥬᏏ ᏏᥬᏏ

Laura's Top 10 Leadership Lessons

1. **Surround yourself with smarties:** Don't be afraid to hire or surround yourself with people who are smarter than you. A good leader isn't threatened by those who excel in areas where they do not. My experience has been that smart people make me look smarter, not dumber.
2. **Keep your financial house in order:** Sometimes we can get so caught up in helping others that we forget to take care of ourselves, in particular our finances. Money and financial problems can pull the rug out from under a great leader. You don't have to be great with your money, just be good enough.
3. **Laugh until you pee a little:** If you aren't laughing, you aren't living. Take time to laugh, but REALLY laugh. Laughter reminds me to not take myself or life too seriously. I consider laughing as part of my self-care. A good laugh keeps me sane.
4. **Believe in yourself:** The only way people will believe in your vision and ideas is if you believe in them yourself and if you believe in your ability to achieve success. Share that passion and demonstrate your commitment to your ideas. Saying something with confidence is just as important as what you are saying. Delivery matters.
5. **Pick your family:** Surround yourself with people who love and care about you and who share your values. Make them your "chosen" family. My chosen family (which I call "The Village") acts as my support system, celebrating my successes and softening my heartbreaks.
6. **Shake your *nalgas*:** Dancing is a quick way to turn a bad mood into a better mood. When I am facing a tough decision or stressing about dealing with a difficult person or situation, I crank the headphones and dance around my office (door closed, of course). Moving my body helps move my mind to a better space.

7. **Honor the past:** It can be easy to dismiss those who came before us because of their old-school ways of organizing and leadership styles. Take time to understand why those leaders were successful in their time and why they continue (or don't continue) to be successful. Take a local leader to coffee or lunch. The stories they tell and advice they give are truly golden.

8. **Give them your *ojo* (no, not THAT kind of *ojo*):** People want to be heard. A good way to show that you are actively listening is to look them in the eye. It seems simple enough, but it can be challenging at a social gathering with lots of people and when the topic of conversation isn't of great interest to you. I try to stay focused on the person in front of me, not those around me. It's much harder than it sounds!

9. **Know your nemesis:** Life is like a movie. There are good characters and bad ones. There will be people you face in life that are just bad, *El Cucuy* bad. Know them, but don't let them control you. Time spent on them is time you don't spend on yourself and the goals you want to achieve.

10. **Remember that the pen is mightier than the sword:** Learn to write well. Words matter, but more importantly, words move people. Writing is like public speaking, you get better by doing it. Try to take time to write a little each day or week.

ROXANNA BARBOZA

Roxanna Barboza was born on May 3, 1996, in Lost Hills, California. She is a first generation Mexican American whose parents are from Guerrero, Mexico. She received a BS in Public Policy and a Master of Public Administration at the University of Southern California. Barboza was a consultant at the US Department of Agriculture supporting their ReConnect Loan and Grant Program in 2019-2020. She is an Industry and Cybersecurity Policy Analyst at National Telephone Cooperative Association (NTCA) of the Rural Broadband Association. Barboza oversees CyberShare, a program that operates as a cyber threat information-sharing and dissemination platform for operators of small telecommunications companies. She also provides expert advice and assistance to member systems and NTCA staff concerning regulatory, competitive and technical issues affecting the rural broadband industry, including cyber security policy. Hailing from California's Central Valley, Barboza has helped address the digital divide in rural areas of the United States.

⁂

Roxanna's Top 10 Leadership Lessons

1. **Be true to yourself.** Follow what your heart desires and run with it because at the end of the day, this is your life, so do what you enjoy.
2. **Be your own hero.** Do not aspire to be anyone but a better version of yourself every day. You are the one who will always be there for yourself.
3. **Network, network, network.** Invest time in building relationships with people that share similar interests. They will help you in the short and long run of your career.
4. **Actively seek constructive feedback.** It may be hard to swallow but that's how you will keep on growing.
5. **Develop work-life balance.** This will help you have a satisfying work and home experience, lessen your stress.
6. **Look forward to the future but be present.** Don't lose focus but be present. You have always wanted to be where you are at, so enjoy it. You will never get this time back.
7. **Don't be afraid to ask questions.** There is no dumb question. Ask away. It is better to know what you are being tasked to do, instead of going around it.
8. **Learn how to say no.** You will be swamped with work and resentful of your situation, which will prohibit you from doing a great job at work.
9. **Take it easy on yourself.** Life is difficult as it is, so don't be harsh on yourself. Be patient, we all have those days and times.
10. **Don't compare yourself.** It's only going to harm you. Understand that everyone has their own path to success so stay in your lane.

SINDY M. BENAVIDES

Sindy Marisol Benavides was born on April 12, 1982 in San Pedro Sula, Honduras and immigrated to the United States in 1983; she is a legal permanent resident in the process of becoming a United States Citizen. She graduated with her Political Science degree from Virginia State University in 2003 and has earned additional education and training from the Boston College Center for Corporate Citizenship-Wells Fargo Academy for Non Profit Leadership; the Hispanas Organized for Political Equality-2018 HOPE National Public Service Fellowship; the 2009 Executive Leadership Program, John F. Kennedy School of Government, Harvard University, among others. Since 2018, Benavides has served as the CEO of the League of United Latin American Citizens (LULAC), the oldest Hispanic civil rights organization in the country. She had previously served as LULAC's Director of Civic Engagement & Community Mobilization. She served as Vice President of Field & Political Operations at Voto Latino Inc., from March 2012-August 2012; as the Northern Virginia Political Director for the Tim Kaine Virginia US Senatorial

Campaign, 2011-2012 and as the National Director of Community Outreach for the Democratic National Committee, 2009-2011. She also as the Director of Gubernatorial Appointments & Latino Liaison, 2006-2009, in the Virginia governor's office. Benavides serves on the boards of various civic and non-profit organizations and on advisory councils for AT&T, Charter Communications, T-Mobile and Verizon. Her most notable awards include the 2021 Crittenton Leadership Award, Crittenton Services of Greater Washington, Top 100 Latina Leaders in Latino Leaders Magazine (2021) and the Visionary Award Honoree from the National Action Network (2020).

⋐⊚ ⊚⋑

Sindy's Top 10 Leadership Lessons

1. **Always choose love:** Every choice we make, no matter how big or small, we either walk towards fear or walk towards love. No matter how scared or fearful, always choose love. Love is what is possible.

2. **Be you:** We must understand where we came from, to understand who we are and where we are going. You are the expert of your lived experiences and only you can narrate your story. Remember to honor your roots and ancestors in all your actions.

3. **Set boundaries:** I'm still learning this one and can honestly admit it's a challenge when it comes to work. However, you need balance, rest and moments for you to be your best in your career. Do it for you.

4. **Speak truth and act:** Early on, I learned that I can't just talk about the change I want to see. I have to be the change. We must be active players in the future we want to see, and that means that you may have to be the person that organizes or starts the movement. What you have to say and what you do matters.

5. **You are worthy:** You are a child of God. Silence the voices in your head and remember that you are enough and worthy. Deconstruct what you have learned and check your own assumptions and biases. You were created with purpose. Fulfill it.

6. **Together we rise:** Influence is the impact that each one of us can have on each other, regardless of background, age, nationality, sexual orientation, gender, religion or even the zip code in which we grew up. As you learn and grow, be a resource to others. Be the connector and inspire others with positive affirmations.

7. **Believe:** Life can be challenging. Our circumstances and lack of exposure can impede us from looking at what is possible and even impede us from harnessing our own potential. Believe in yourself firmly and create a vison board of what you want with a realistic timeline. We are the chief architects of our journeys, and it will be up to us to propose the next solution that will radically shift the way we think and do business.

8. **Be financially savvy:** Learn early on how to budget, save and invest. We must create financial stability to be able to focus on the bigger picture. Being financially stable will allow you to experience freedom in your choices.

9. **Learn the lesson(s):** Moving mountains and walking on bumpy roads are part of the journey. When you experience hard times in your life, take time to reflect and learn from the moment. Grow from the dark valleys you cross because you were meant to cross them and not live in them eternally.

10. **Challenge the status quo:** We must change our mindset and even unlearn what we have read in books or what we see on TV and read on social media, which omit our own voices, narratives, experiences and journeys. When a table is not big enough for all to be seated, we must speak up and acknowledge the biases in the rules and systems that leave us out because they were not originally created with women and people of color in mind.

MARIA ANTONIA "TONI" BERRIOS

Maria Antonia "Toni" Berrios was born on April 24, 1977, in Chicago, Illinois to Puerto Rican parents. She received her undergraduate degree from Northeastern Illinois University and earned her MBA with a concentration on International Business from Keiser University. Berros is the president of MAB Strategies, Inc., a consulting company in Illinois. She served six terms in the Illinois General Assembly as the representative from the Northwest Side Chicago. In 2002, she became the first Puerto Rican woman to serve in the Illinois House of Representatives and the first second-generation Latina state representative, following in her father's footsteps, who was the first Latino elected to the Illinois General Assembly, in 1982. During her tenure in Springfield, Berrios served as chair of the Board of Hispanic Caucus Chairs (2014), a national Latino legislative leadership organization, and chair of the Illinois Legislative Latino Caucus and Foundation (2014). She is a co-founder of the National Latina State Legislative Caucus of the Board of Latino Legislative Leaders.

உௌ ௫

Toni's Top 10 Leadership Lessons

1. **Your word is your bond:** When you tell someone you are going to support them or their issue, stand behind your word.
2. **Family first:** Your family believes in you enough to support you and stand by your side. Always make time for them too.
3. **Just ask:** You do not know everything about every topic, and you don't have to. There is always help around you. Just ask for it.
4. **Never shy away from hard work**: Running for office, passing laws, listening to the community and hosting events is hard work; it builds character and shows strength.
5. **Always give back:** Volunteer with nonprofits and different organizations whenever you can; mentor others and help without expecting anything in return.
6. **Never forget where you came from:** No matter how humble your beginning, always remember that it's a part of you and only makes you stronger.
7. **Stand your ground:** Many issues and situations come your way at once. When you know it's the right thing to do, don't let others sway what you believe is correct.
8. **Have your "Bonita Caucus":** Surround yourself with women who believe in the same things you believe in and who will fight alongside you and mentor you.
9. **Be resilient and believe in yourself:** Sometimes life's challenges knock you down. It's up to you to stand back up, dust off and move forward.
10. **Self-care:** As women, we take care of everyone else before ourselves. Remember to always make time for you!

YESENIA CALDERÓN

Yesenia Calderón was born on August 17, 1990, in Rocky Mount, North Carolina to Mexican immigrant parents who were farm-workers. Her family followed the harvest in communities across North Carolina and Florida twice a year. She received her bachelor's degree in English from the University of Central Florida in 2014 and her JD from the Nova Southeastern University Shepard Broad College of Law in 2018. She works as an immigration attorney at the Children's Legal Program at Americans for Immigrant Rights in Florida, where she represents immigrant children, many of whom have suffered abuse, abandonment or neglect. In 2014, Yesenia was selected for the National Migrant and Seasonal Head Start Association (NMSHSA) Summer Internship in Washington, DC and was placed at the Mexican American Legal Defense and Education Fund. Yesenia was featured on NBC Nightly News during her NMSHSA Summer Internship.

cᴐꙆ Ɠᴑ

Yesenia's Top 10 Leadership Lessons

1. **Create your own happiness:** Figure out what people, places, things and activities make your soul feel like it's on fire. Life is hectic but it's also way too short, so live like you were dying. And go create your own happiness!

2. **Create strong relationships:** Yes, mentorship is very important, but I am referring to relationships that surpass the act of guidance. Create strong relationships with people that you can be silly around, show your weaknesses, grief and vulnerabilities. Those are the relationships that survive anything and last a lifetime.

3. **Be grateful:** For the past several years, I write down ten things I am grateful for every night before I go to bed—even the smallest of things, like a warm cup of coffee or a beautiful sunset. Studies have shown that grateful people are happier, live longer and even feel healthier.

4. **Define your meaning of success:** Success is something you must define for yourself. It has a different meaning for every person. Some define it as money and power, while others define it as a career or title. I always have and will continue to define success as happiness.

5. **Be fully present:** Fully enjoy the moment you are in. Time is passing by, so pay attention and listen.

6. **Learn from your failures:** When you fail, because you will, take it as a learning experience. Ask yourself, what can I learn from this? Use your answer as a stepping stone.

7. **No "what ifs":** Live your life with no "what ifs." Take risks! Be bold!

8. **Strong healthy habits:** Make sure you are giving your body what it needs to lead: exercise, water, healthy food and sleep.

9. **Ready, set, goal:** Set short-term and long-term goals. Write them down and look at them often. Celebrate all of them . . . even the tiniest one!

10. **Pray, pray, pray:** I pray every morning because I believe that there is a God and believe in the power of prayer. Prayer helps me with anxiety and stress. If you feel uncomfortable praying, you can meditate instead.

YOLANDA CAMARENA

Yolanda Camarena, a second-generation Mexican American, was born on August 18, 1955, in San Antonio, Texas. She obtained her bachelor's degree in Education from Wichita State University in 1978 and her Master in Public Administration from the John F. Kennedy School of Government at Harvard University in 1988. She has two daughters, Gena and Marisa, and her husband is Gene Camarena. Camarena serves as Vice President of Camarena Adelante Foundation and is a trustee for Newman University in Wichita, Kansas. She also serves on the Board of the Kansas Hispanic Education and Development Foundation; she previously served on the Wichita Community Foundation from 2015-2021. She is the chair of the Schools and Scholarship Committee of Harvard College and the Hispanic Scholarship Fund Advisory Committee. She served as the associate director of Graduate Programs at the Kennedy School of Government at Harvard University from 1983 to 1988. During her time at Harvard, she and several Latino graduate students co-founded the *Harvard Journal of Hispanic Policy* in 1985. Upon her return to Wichita, she served as the Regional Coordinator for the LULAC Educational Service Center from 1989 to 1993. Her most notable awards include the Inclusion in Entrepreneurship Award by Create Campaign, Inc. in 2021, the selection for the Business Hall of Fame of Junior Achievement in 2020, the Outstanding Philanthropist Award of the *Wichita Business Journal* in 2019 and the Lifetime Achievement Award of the Wichita Hispanic Chamber of Commerce in 2016. She was awarded an honorary Doctor of Humane Letters from Newman University in 2015.

⚬⚬ ⚬⚬

Yolanda's Top 10 Leadership Lessons

1. ***"Dios te lo multiplicará"*:** My mother always said this to us for as long as I can remember. We were taught to always give to others because God would multiply our blessings. We all have something to give or share with others, but what we receive in return is far greater than what we give. Just remember, "*Dios te lo multiplicará.*"

2. **Put on your oxygen mask first:** Flight attendants always tell you to put on your oxygen mask first before helping others. This means you have to take care of what you need to do in your life. Complete your education, start your career, gain some wealth and then you will be in a better position to help others. It doesn't mean you can't do something now; it means you can do more later.

3. **Going from the barrio to the boardroom:** Always remember who you are, where you started from and where you want to go. Complete your education, get your work experience and find the mentors who will guide you to that seat at the boardroom table. Take your seat and make your voice heard. That's where change can begin, and don't forget to hold a seat for someone else.

4. **Be a cheerleader:** Pick up your pompoms and cheer the loudest for your daughters, sisters, women co-workers or whomever is important to you. Be that voice of encouragement, positive energy, faith and love. Sometimes all someone needs is to hear from the sidelines, "GO, FIGHT, WIN!"

5. **Always be learning and growing:** If you're not learning or being challenged in your career, organization or life, it's time to make a change. Don't become complacent because you will no longer be productive or happy. Find that project no one wants, lead the next meeting, organize a community event and be a leader. Change is uncomfortable sometimes, but in the end you did it, and it usually isn't as bad as you thought.

6. **Self-confidence can be a superpower:** Self-confidence gives you the strength to make tough decisions, pick yourself back up when knocked down and live to fight another day. So put on your cape, look at yourself in the mirror and, as my good friend Delia García would say, "I'm a *chingona*!"

7. **Manage your own career:** If you're not managing your career, someone else is, and you might not like the results. You want to manage your career like you manage your money. You want to grow, diversify and, most importantly, invest in yourself. You are your best asset!

8. **Define success on your own terms:** You don't need to compare yourself to others. You should define who you are by what is important in your life, what you have achieved and what you still plan to accomplish. This will define your success.

9. **Choose a life partner:** Whom we choose as a life partner is very important. This person will be your better half in life and in building a family. Will they support, respect and make you a better person or will they be an anchor and bring you down in the end? The choice is yours to make, so choose wisely.

10. **Create your own legacy:** No matter how much time we spend on this Earth, we create our own legacy. Some aspects of your legacy will be positive and others negative. How will you be remembered? I hope to be remembered for doing good for others and honoring God. If you have the opportunity to have an impact on one life during your time on Earth—one life matters—you will have a significant impact on this journey we call life. Make it count.

CARMEN CANTOR

Carmen Cantor was born on February 23, 1968, in Mayagüez, Puerto Rico. She earned a BA in Sociology from the University of Puerto Rico, Mayagüez Campus, in 1989, and an MA in Labor Relations from the Inter American University of Puerto Rico in 1993. She attended executive courses at Harvard University's Kennedy School of Government and the Center for Creative Leadership, the Air War College and other programs. She is also an alumna of the National Hispana Leadership Institute Executive Leadership Program and the Aspen Institute's International Career Advancement Program. She is a career member of the Senior Executive Service and has been the US Ambassador to the Federated States of Micronesia since 2019. From 2016 to 2019, she served as director of the Office of Civil Service Human Resource Management in the Bureau of Human Resources, the executive director for the Bureaus of Educational and Cultural Affairs and International Information Programs from 2013 to 2015 and the executive director of the Bureau of Counterterrorism (CT) at the US Department of State from 2011 to 2013. Before rejoining the Department of State, Carmen worked as director of the Office of Civil Rights at the Foreign Agricultural Service and Director of the Office of Equal Employment Opportunity of the US Federal Maritime Commission in Washington, DC. During her career, she received the Secretary of State's Equal Employment Opportunity Award, a Superior Honor Award for her outstanding performance as the first executive director in the Counterterrorism Bureau and a Meritorious Honor Award for outstanding performance and for providing inspiring leadership and management in the Bureau of Human Resources' Office of Recruitment. In May of 2014, *Latina Style* magazine named her one of five Latina Trailblazers of American Foreign Policy at the US Department of State.

ເໆ໑ ໑ນ

Carmen's Top 10 Leadership Lessons

1. **Never stop learning:** Work on your college degree, but don't stop there. Take continuing education classes, executive courses and leadership training. No one can take your credentials from you.
2. **Be persistent and brave:** Have courage and don't pay too much attention to your inner critic. Be firm, in spite of challenges.
3. **Champion your own career:** Advocate for yourself, win support from others and find mentors and sponsors.
4. **Be a talent agent and support other women:** Coach, mentor, develop and elevate other women. Advocate for them.
5. **Be self-aware, be yourself and be humble:** Know your strengths and your value, but also your areas for improvement and limitations. Focus on your strengths. Acknowledge your mistakes and learn from them.
6. **Take care of yourself:** You have to make the time! Have an annual physical test, exercise daily and learn something new, such as a hobby or a sport. Find ways to decompress.
7. **Always dress for the next job you want:** Some people call it "Dress for Success." Have a professional look all the time.
8. **Have executive presence:** This is not about your wardrobe; it's about showing determination, regardless of your current position. It's the ability to inspire confidence!
9. **Embrace change:** Get uncomfortable, adapt to change, be flexible.
10. **Establish a strong professional network:** Build alliances, find a place to connect and communicate with others. Networks will provide opportunities to thrive.

ANGELA CERVANTES

Angela Cervantes was born and raised in Kansas City, Kansas, and chooses not to share her date of birth. She is a second-generation Mexican American/Chicana and the granddaughter of immigrants. She earned her BA in English Literature from the University of Kansas in Lawrence, Kansas, and her MBA from Avila University in Kansas City, Missouri. Cervantes is the author of several children's novels, including *American Girl Book Maritza: Lead With Your Heart* (2021); *Lety Out Loud*, named the 2020 Pura Belpré Honor Book by the American Library Association; *Gaby, Lost and Found*; *Allie, First At Last*; and the mystery novel, *Me, Frida and the Secret of the Peacock Ring*. Angela also wrote the junior novelization of Disney Pixar's animated films, *Coco* and *Encanto* (2021). Angela began writing stories featuring Latina main characters when she was nine years old because she wanted books about her friends and Mexican-American community and heritage. She has served as an author mentor for such organizations as We Need Diverse Books and Las Musas in order to help other Latina writers navigate the publishing universe.

⟨♒ ♒⟩

Angela's Top 10 Leadership Lessons

1. **Create a mission statement:** Post it up on your desk or somewhere you can see it every day. Always check your actions with this mission.
2. **Share your mission:** If the folks around you don't know what you're trying to achieve, how can they support you? I've found that when I shared my dream to be a published author with others, many people stepped up to help and support me by offering connections, opportunities and words of encouragement.
3. **Surround yourself with smart and positive people:** Be brave enough to step away from those who'd rather complain and destroy joy.
4. **Don't let the ugliness in others kill the beauty in you:** Never let the haters bring you down. Stay focused on your goals and keep moving.
5. **Learn to say no:** Everyone will want your time and attention. Be selfish about your priorities and time. Don't be afraid to say no to things that are distractions from your mission.
6. **Never stop being a student:** Every day is an opportunity to learn more and ask questions.
7. **Always be grateful:** I have opportunities that my *abuelos* never had. Their life and work make my life as a writer possible. I'm forever grateful. Gratitude guides me every day.
8. **Recognize other leaders:** Being a Latina leader is tough. Back other Latinas up by sharing knowledge, opportunities and praise!
9. **Know your limits:** It's totally okay to step back from taking the lead to make time for yourself. You're not stopping. You're recharging.
10. **Rewrite, rewrite, rewrite!** When things get difficult, rewrite the struggle as a challenge, not as a catastrophe.

JOANNA CIFREDO

Joanna Cifredo was born on February 9, 1987, in Bayamón, Puerto Rico. She is a student of Sustainable Development and Political Science at the Universidad del Sagrado Corazón in San Juan, Puerto Rico, and is a transgender human rights activist. Cifredo has spent her career uplifting the voices of transgender people across the United States and Latin America while working to improve public policy to address the inequities facing trans communities. She currently leads as a grassroots community organizer, policy analyst and media coach. Her work centers around expanding educational opportunities and healthcare access to marginalized communities, particularly trans communities. Joanna has received numerous awards, including the 2015 Rising Star Award of the Mujeres en el Movimiento, the 2015 Visionary Voice Award of the National Sexual Violence Resource Center and the 2015 Poderosa a Velar of the National Latina Institute for Reproductive Health.

⤾⤿

Joanna's Top 10 Leadership Lessons

1. **Think big and in HD:** Everything you see around you started as a thought in someone's mind. In order to be a good leader, first think about what kind of leader you want to be. You can be a leader and not be leading your team anywhere.
2. **Have an idea of where you want to go:** You don't necessarily need to know all the details of exactly how to get there, that's what your team is for, but you do need to have a vision of what your team is collectively working towards.
3. **Learn to be transparent:** Don't be afraid to let your team know what's up. Be human in front of your team. This will help foster a culture of openness.
4. **Even when it's about you, it's not about you:** True leadership is about holding the space for the brilliance of others. Even if you might be the figurehead of your organization, it's important to remember that everyone plays an essential part.
5. **Show gratitude:** Whether it's in a thank you note, taking someone out for lunch or a small kind gesture, people are always willing to go the extra mile for a boss who is appreciative.
6. **Meditate in the mornings:** I can't stress meditating in the mornings for 5 to 10 mins enough, especially before you look at your phone. You will literally have a different nervous system and different day if you do.
7. **Be your team's hype person:** Imposter syndrome is real, and you're probably not the only one struggling with it. Affirming your team members' good attributes will help establish a positive workplace culture.

8. **Look at "failure" differently:** Sometimes things don't work out for one reason or another. This might just be an unexpected detour that helps you arrive at your original destination quicker than you expected.

9. **Lead with integrity:** Be of good faith and honesty, and things will always work themselves out.

10. **Remember joy:** Joy is a necessary component in fighting for justice.

LUPITA COLMENERO

Lupita Colmenero was born on December 20, 1962, in San Diego de la Union, Guanajuato, Mexico. She became a US citizen on July 17, 1999. She obtained a degree in Social Work from the Universidad Autónoma de México, Mexico City, in 1982, is a graduate of the Tuck Minority Business Enterprise Program (2007) and the Executive Leadership Development Program HACR at Harvard University (2006). Colmenero is the co-founder and publisher of *El Hispano News,* in Dallas, Texas and the COO of LATINA *Style* Inc. She is also the president and founder of Parents Step Ahead (PSA), a Dallas-based nonprofit that works to "recognize, educate, enable and empower parents to take a proactive role in the educational and personal development of their children." In 2005, she was the first woman elected president of the National Association of Hispanic Publications Inc. Among her awards are the Woman of the Year of *Solo Mujeres Magazine* (2020), the Living Legend Award of the Hispanic 100 Dallas (2019) and the Coors Líderes (2007).

ഏ ഔ

Lupita's Top 10 Leadership Lessons

1. **Believe in yourself:** Start by acknowledging that you are not perfect (nobody is), and then set your mind to accomplish anything you can think of. The worse obstacles in life are the ones we put in front of ourselves (consciously and unconsciously). Love yourself, respect yourself and believe in yourself, and you should be able to embrace failure and success in total harmony.

2. **If you want to go fast, go alone. If you want to go far, go together:** We can be as strong as we want to be, but never enough to do it alone. The best we can do is rely on the power and contribution of others. Do not be afraid to ask for help and ask someone to be your mentor, your coach. Be mindful of its value and nurture it; make them feel proud of you. Don't forget to pay it forward! Be a mentor too; search for mentees and pass on the baton with the gift of wisdom you received.

3. **Learn to be quiet:** When you get into a conversation or argument with someone, make sure your purpose is not to win but to learn from it. Give people the value and respect they deserve by listening to what they have to say and share. And if you don't like what they say, before you ignore it, try to visualize yourself in their position and find the balance that will still allow you to take something good from that experience.

4. **Dissolve mountains into sand and sunbathe on it:** Start by eliminating all the "ifs" and "buts" in your life (even from your vocabulary) and wipe out all the little things that constantly say that this and that cannot be achieved, whether it is personal or professional. "Where there is a will, there is a way." You have what it takes to make it happen. If you don't know how, learn how.

5. **Find your pack:** "Tell me who your friends are, and I'll tell you who you are." We can mingle and interact with many. But if we are not mindful, intentional and organized about those relationships, then we are missing opportunities. Cultivate new contacts into fruitful relationships; don't waste valuable opportunities. Remember: in order to cultivate fruitful relationships, you also need to reciprocate. Life is a two-way road. Give and receive. Receive and give.

6. **You were born to succeed:** Understand and accept that no one is exempt from failure, pain and loss. Those experiences are part of life; so, to understand them, we need go through them first. We must be able to recognize and acknowledge failures, and only then can we learn and grow. At the end it is a matter of choice; it is not an easy one, but it is up to us to choose the route we take.

7. **Work on building yourself and also building others:** Imagine the life you want to live, the partner you want to share it with and the type of job you want to do and enjoy, then start building the road that will take you there. Don't allow the casualties of life deter you from that route. Do "checks and balances" routinely on all the stops and turns your road has, and make sure it is still taking you to your desired destination. There may be stops that you need to make to keep building on your purpose, and that is okay as long as you are mindful and intentional about your main goal. Make sure you also lift others on your way there.

8. **Don't suffer life's turns twice:** Anything you set your mind to achieve is possible (not easy but possible), and it is up to you to conquer it. Liberate yourself of feelings that don't enrich your mind, soul and body and then set yourself to fly and conquer everything you dream of. Get close only to people who share your values, principles and ideas. Don't invest time and energy in those who don't. Don't think or worry about bad outcomes, much less before they happen. "Don't worry. Be happy!"

9. **Count your blessing:** Be humble, compassionate and grant others the same respect you deserve. You are special because you decide to be that way, because of the work, the principle and values you decide to apply and abide by. You are special because you earn it with self-discipline and self-respect and respect for others.

10. **You are a miracle:** Yes, you are! Believe it! We all are miracles. We conquered many battles even before we were born, and each of us has a mission. So, love yourself first and foremost, physically and mentally! Because that is the only way you will be able to take care of and truly love those around you. Meditate, read, dance, sing and laugh (even if everyone is watching)!

FRANCES COLÓN

Frances Colón was born on October 31, 1974, in Puerto Rico. She earned her BS in Biology in 1997 from the University of Puerto Rico and her PhD in Neuroscience in 2004 from Brandeis University. Colón was appointed to the Biden Administration President's Council of Advisors on Science and Technology and serves as the Senior Director for International Climate at the Center for American Progress. She currently specializes in advising on science policy and evidence-based decision-making for governments. Colón has also been president of Jasperi Consulting since 2017 and is the former Deputy Science and Technology Adviser to the US Secretary of State. As an Open Society Foundations 2019 Leadership in Government Fellow, Colón worked to catalyze policy action to counter the impacts of climate change on vulnerable communities in Florida. She has received numerous awards and recognitions, including the Latino National Security & Foreign Policy Next Generation Leaders 2020 Award, the Top 100 Influential Latinas in *Latino Leaders Magazine* (2020), the New Voices of the National Academies of Science (2019-2020), the Cnet-20 Most Influential Latinos in Technology (2016) and the Hispanic Heritage Foundation Inspire Award (2015).

ᥨᥩ ᥩᥢ

Frances' Top 10 Leadership Lessons

1. **Empowering others is the key to success:** The success of your team, each individual member reaching full potential, is how you achieve your mission.
2. **Never stop learning:** We have so many directions we can still grow in. Be vulnerable and let the transformation take place.
3. **With adversity, comes resilience:** Embrace challenge as the door to the new path you had not considered, to the change that makes you stronger.
4. **We are the ones we have been waiting for:** Every moment in life is a chance to innovate and have impact. Wait for no one; it is up to you.
5. **Speak your truth:** Your voice, your experience and your perspective are unique and of value to the world we are trying to change for the better.
6. **Do the overlooked task:** The greatest opportunities can come from taking on the project everyone shuns and making it the greatest success they have ever seen. It will become the next must-do and must-be.
7. **Bring compassion:** Lead from a place of understanding of the humanity and potential of those you are seeking to inspire. There is greatness, lived experience, pain and joy in all of us.
8. **Give more than you take:** Be generous with growth opportunities for others, and abundance will follow.
9. **Listen first:** Your talents and ideas will find their best home if you listen carefully to what is needed.
10. **Be nimble:** Adaptability and an open mind enrich us with the flexibility to go beyond the bar that has been set.

CARMEN YULÍN CRUZ SOTO

Carmen Yulín Cruz Soto was born on February 25, 1963, in San Juan, Puerto Rico. She graduated with a BA in Liberal Arts from Boston University in 1984 and obtained a Master in Public Policy from Carnegie Mellon University in 1986. She was elected in 2008 as representative at-large for the Puerto Rico House of Representatives. In 2012, was elected mayor of San Juan and re-elected in 2016. She rose to national fame for her heroic efforts to restore life to Puerto Rico after Hurricane María and, for her efforts, was named to *Time* magazine's 100 Most Influential People in the World (2018) and received the Martin Luther King Centre Justice Award (2018), the Peace and Freedom Award and Humanitarian Leadership Award (2018), the Antonio Villaraigosa Leadership Award (2018), among many others. Boston University conferred an honorary Doctor of Laws to Mayor Cruz in May 2020. In February 2019, the United States Hispanic Leadership Institute presented Mayor Cruz with the Dolores Huerta Woman of Courage Medallion.

❦ ❧

Carmen Yulín's Top 10 Leadership Lessons

1. **Magnify voices:** A leader uses her platform to magnify the voices of those without a platform.
2. **True leadership is everywhere:** A leader understands that leadership is not given by titles or positions, but that true leadership can be found in the most unexpected places.
3. **The power of one voice:** A leader never underestimates one voice as irrelevant, for she understands that one true voice can quickly summon the power of many voices.
4. **See solutions and opportunities:** A leader can see solutions where others see problems, and sees opportunities where others see obstacles.
5. **It is okay to ask for help:** A leader knows when to ask for help.
6. **Create common platforms:** A leader understands her role in engaging a diversity of voices to work together and create common platforms, which in turn liberate other voices to strive for hope, respect and equality.
7. **You can make mistakes:** You can make mistakes while doing something to try and solve a problem, rather than not making mistakes because you are scared to fail.
8. **Be prepared for any crisis at any point:** Leadership is about being prepared to face crises because sooner or later you will face at least one.
9. **Speak truth to power:** Understand that when faced with a crisis one has two options: stand up and speak truth to power or stand down and become complicit to a narrative which will perpetuate the crisis.
10. **Help others connect the dots of the human spirit:** So that we can all reach our potential, no matter who we are, no matter what that looks like.

VICTORIA DEFRANCESCO SOTO

Victoria DeFrancesco Soto was born on April 27, 1978, in Sierra Vista, Arizona. She received her BA in Political Science and Latin American Studies from the University of Arizona in 2000 and a PhD in Political Science in American Politics from Duke University in 2007. She is currently the dean of The Clinton School of Public Service at the University of Arkansas. Previously, she served as the assistant dean of Civic Engagement at the Lyndon Baines Johnson School of Public Affairs at The University of Texas in Austin (2012-2021). Prior to working in administration, she taught at Rutgers University and Northwestern University (2007-2011). Underlying all of her research interests is the intersection of social group identity and political participation. Since 2012, DeFrancesco Soto has served as a contributor to MSNBC and NBCNews.com and has served as a political analyst for Telemundo. In 2011, she was named to *Diverse* magazine's Top 10 Scholars in Minority Academics.

⌒◌⊙ ⊙◌⌒

Victoria's Top 10 Leadership Lessons

1. **Listen:** God gave us two ears and one mouth. Leadership isn't about speaking the most or the loudest; it's about being the most informed when speaking.
2. *El que se enoja, pierde* **(if you get mad, you lose):** This doesn't mean suppress your feelings; just don't let them show. Get out your frustration with your inner circle and then keep your eye on the prize.
3. **Value your ride or it dies:** These are the people who love you, not because of your position or what you can do for them, but because of who you are; these are your childhood friends, *tías*, loved ones. Never neglect them, they will keep you grounded.
4. **The truth hurts:** When something bothers you deeply, analyze why that is. Don't automatically ignore or blame others. Understand why you are so bothered and figure out how to address the issue at the core.
5. **Don't put something on social media (or e-mail) that you wouldn't want splashed on the front page of a major newspaper site or website:** For better or worse, perception is reality.
6. **Don't be a room scanner:** When you are at an event, pay attention to the person in front of you. Listen and value people, regardless of their title.
7. **Embrace your nervousness:** Being nervous before any big event is natural. Embrace those nerves and have them give you power. Don't let them take away your power.
8. **Listen to what people are *not* saying:** True leadership requires thoughtful listening and observation. Many times, the non-verbal cues, or silence, are as important as what people are saying.

9. **Have your walk-on song:** The best way to channel nervous energy into excitement is by having a "kick-a" walk-on song. Listen to it while you're getting ready and right before you go "on."

10. **There's always a silver lining, always:** Leadership is about engaging with crisis. However, the mark of effective leadership is figuring out how to grow from crises and setbacks.

CRISANTA DURAN

Crisanta Duran was born on August 23, 1980, in Boulder, Colorado, and is a sixth generation Coloradan with Mexican and Native American ancestry. She graduated from the University of Denver with a double major in Public Policy and Spanish in 2002, the University of Colorado School of Law in 2005 and the Harvard Kennedy School Executives in Government program in 2017. She served in the Colorado House of Representatives from 2011 to 2019 and was the first Latina to serve as the Speaker of the House. Duran has served as a board member of Let America Vote, the National Association of Latino/a Elected and Appointed Officials, the National Board of Hispanic Caucus Chairs and as a member of the National Latina State Legislative Caucus. She is a National Co-Chair of the Voto Latino Impact Council. In 2020, she wrote a report to the Denver Police about being beaten and raped prior to becoming Speaker of the House, believing she was targeted to weaken her before she took on this important position. Duran has received numerous awards for her leadership, including the national Emily's List Rising Star Award in 2016, the

Aspen Institute's Rodel Public Leadership Fellowship, the Colorado Women's Chamber of Commerce Top 25 Most Powerful Women Award in 2018, the Conservation Colorado Legislator of the Year Award in 2014, the Dr. Martin Luther King Jr. Humanitarian Award in 2016 and the United Veterans Committee of Colorado Distinguished Service Award.

ભિ ભ

Crisanta's Top 10 Leadership Lessons

1. **Work collectively:** It is powerful when people come together to make change. Work to collectively unite others towards a common goal by considering the lens that they look through.
2. **Minimize regrets:** We must all die someday. Take action to do what's right when you have the opportunity to do so to minimize regrets when that day will come.
3. **Know your worth:** Don't allow others to use shame or stigma to determine your worth or your role to lead.
4. **Be aware of status quo systems:** Be aware of status quo systems that have prevented progress of underserved communities. Consider giving a voice to the voiceless and the people who are left out of the decision-making process before coming to final conclusions.
5. **Stand still and see yourself:** Take time to reflect about everything that's happening around you.
6. **Believe yourself *poderosa*:** One person's voice can move mountains. Believe in yourself and your ability to make a difference.
7. **Emphasize a culture of appreciation:** White supremacy promotes a perfectionist culture that relies on guilt, fear and shame as motivators for work. Emphasize a culture of appreciation in which people's work is recognized and valued.
8. **Enjoy being a winner and a learner:** There are times when people may feel lost, but they have actually won. Enjoy the journey and learn from all experiences regardless of outcome.

9. **Be an equity fighter:** Many people say they support the principles of equity, until they have something to lose. Fight for equity anyways.

10. **Build a support tribe:** There are few permanent friends and permanent enemies in the world of politics. Build a tribe of support that will be there regardless of whether they benefit or not from the relationship.

INGRID M. DURAN

Ingrid M. Duran was born on January 13, 1966, in Los Angeles, California. She earned a BS in Science Organizational Management from Park University in 1993 and later studied in Harvard's University John F. Kennedy School of Government Executive Program in 2002 and the Harvard Business School in Corporate Governance Program in 2005. Duran is a former Marine (1986-1989) who is now the CEO and co-founder of D&P Creative Strategies. Prior to starting her own business in 2004, she served as the Congressional Hispanic Caucus Institute President and CEO from 1998 to 2004, and the director of the National Association of Latino Elected & Appointed Officials from 1996 to 1998. A skilled advocate for both the public and private sectors, she builds on her experience to yield solutions that move the needle in modern and innovative ways. Duran played a key role in changing the narrative around gay marriage and ultimately contributed to the landmark Supreme Court case granting equal marriage rights for all. Her efforts as a strong, steadfast leader and advocate for the LGBTQ+ and Latinx communities have garnered her national accolades and numerous honors, including in December 2001, the US Department of Health and Human Services Certificate of Commendation for Service on the President's Advisory Council on HIV/AIDS. Among her other accolades are the Premio Dignidad Award from the National Latina/o Lesbian, Gay, Bisexual and Transgender Organization (2003), named to the 100 Most Influential and Powerful Hispanics by *Hispanic* magazine (2003), The National Gay and Lesbian Task Force 2012 Leadership Award and the *Working Mother Magazine*'s Legacy Award (2013).

cතඐ ඐවා

Ingrid's Top 10 Leadership Lessons

1. **Live your authentic life:** Be true to yourself and others. Embrace your differences.
2. **Never forget where you come from:** Embrace your roots and those who paved the way before you.
3. **Always give back:** Give back to your community, help others along the way.
4. **Give 100% at ALL times:** Always do your best and over-deliver; your work ethic speaks to your character. Don't half step!
5. **Embrace diversity:** Diversity of thought, diversity of background, diversity of differences.
6. **Celebrate your successes:** Celebrate your accomplishments, no matter how big or small.
7. **Learn from failure:** Failure should be embraced and learned from; it teaches us and helps us grow.
8. **Mentor others:** Help others to grow and succeed; share your knowledge freely.
9. **Empower others:** Support others; celebrate their success and achievements.
10. **Don't let fear get in your way:** Fear is a strong emotion; acknowledge it and overcome it. Don't let it impede your success. Believe in yourself.

LUZ ESCAMILLA

Luz Escamilla was born on February 4, 1978, in Mexico City, Mexico, and became a naturalized US citizen on November 8, 2005. Luz grew up in Mexico and, during her last two years of high school, she crossed the border every day to attend high school in San Diego, California. After graduation, she moved to Utah, where she graduated with a BS Science Business Marketing in 2000 and a earned her Master in Public Administration from the University of Utah in 2005. Escamilla has served as a Utah State senator since 2008; she is the senate Minority Whip. In 2020 she became the COO of MiCARE, a medical healthcare management startup company. She had previously worked for more than thirteen years in the banking industry, mainly at Zions Bank, where she served as vice president of the Community Development Group (2013-2020), Hispanic/Latino market manager (2010-2013) and director of Zions Bank's Business Resource Center (2007-2010). Escamilla serves on numerous boards and commissions related to health care, arts and culture. Luz is a member of the National Association of Latino/a Elected and Appointed Officials and the National Latina State Legislative Caucus of the Board of Latino Legislative Leaders. Her awards include the Children's Service Society of Utah Children's Advocacy Award (2019), the Salt Lake Chamber of Commerce New Pioneers American Dream Award (2018), the UCLR César Chávez Peace and Justice Award (2017), the LULAC National Legislator Service Award (2013) and the US Small Business Administration/Minority Small Business Champion of the Year Award (2010).

ᘓᕰ ᕱᘐ

Luz's Top 10 Leadership Lessons

1. **Don't wait for someone to ask you:** You know best when you are ready; you don't need others' permission. Just do it!!
2. **Surround yourself with good people:** *"Dime con quién andas y te diré quién eres"*: the ones that surround you can make you stronger or weaker. Be selective of whom you share your journey, time and dreams with.
3. **Seek and be a mentor/sponsor:** We all need help; asking for help is critical. Don't be too shy to ask for mentorship; at the same time, recognize your privileges and use them to mentor or sponsor others.
4. **You don't have to follow the norm; it's okay to be different:** Be disruptive. You don't have to fit into a norm that doesn't include you and your community. Being different is a plus; it changes the conversation and brings real change.
5. **You really must want it:** Life is full of challenges. Wanting to accomplish things requires a full commitment. Don't be afraid of the power of wanting something with all your heart and will.
6. **Find your center:** Find what motivates you in life, what is your drive. For me, my center is *mi familia.*
7. **Live and enjoy every minute like it is the last one:** Life is short. Be happy and grateful for what you have.
8. **Listen to your inner voice:** Your inner voice guides from your heart; there is wisdom in your heart. Listen to that voice.
9. **Failure and disappointment are a part of success.**
10. **Take care of yourself so you can help others:** Love yourself! In order to effectively serve others and be an successful leader, you have to take care of yourself first. Nurture your body and soul on a regular basis. Nothing is more important than loving yourself. Before you can love others, you have to love and accept yourself for who you are.

CLAUDIA FLORES

Claudia Flores was born on October 23, 1990, in Tegucigalpa, Honduras. She immigrated to the United States as a teenager and grew up in San Jose, California with her immigrant family. She earned her BS in Political Science from Santa Clara University in 2012. Flores currently serves as the associate director of Immigration Policy and Strategy at the Center for American Progress, one of the country's most prominent progressive think tanks, where she has led the issue of immigration since 2017. Prior to that, she led the immigration policy portfolio for the National Latina Institute for Reproductive Health, where she worked on advancing federal and state legislation to expand health care access for immigrant children and families. She also worked on Capitol Hill to advance federal policy relating to matters of immigration enforcement and protections for immigrant youth. Flores is an alumna of the Congressional Hispanic Caucus Institute Fellows Program and the New Leaders Council Fellows Program. Among her most notable recognitions are being selected for the We Lead: Women & Politics Institute at American University

School of Public Affairs Program (2020), the 40 Under 40 Award of Prospanica DC (2019) and the Inter-American Development Bank Young Social Innovator Award. In 2021, she received the Washingtonian's Most Influential People in Washington, DC and the Congressional Hispanic Caucus Institute Young Alumnus Award.

ﻌﻮ ﻮﻮ

Claudia's Top 10 Leadership Lessons

1. **Write down your goals:** Goals help us become the best version of ourselves. By writing down your goals you are able to clarify priorities, set intentions and ultimately measure your progress.
2. **Self-belief:** Have confidence in your talents and purpose. A leader with self-belief knows their worth and value. Life circumstances may affect how you feel about yourself at any given moment; so it is important to build the habit of recognizing the real value of who you are: a leader.
3. **Tell the truth:** Truth builds trust, and trust builds cooperation. Leaders who tell the truth are able to confront reality, which is necessary and worthwhile in making decisions. Truth-telling also defines character; when you walk in your truth, nobody will be able to use it against you or define who you are.
4. **Let yourself be vulnerable:** Vulnerability allows you to check in with yourself, clarifying strong emotions and paving the way for meaningful connections. Leaders who are able to share their experiences in an authentic, vulnerable matter are more likely to foster inclusion.
5. **Take responsibility:** As a leader, you have the opportunity to effect positive change in the lives of others. When you take the step of accepting a leadership role, you recognize the need for change and welcome an opportunity to give voice to your values. Act responsibly.
6. **Let failure guide you:** How you approach failure defines your next steps. My biggest failures have given me the opportunity to start again, and that has made all the difference in moving past stagnation.

7. **Run together:** As I crossed the finish line after running my first race, I felt a deep sense of accomplishment and gratitude. I was in awe of the distance that I had achieved and grateful for the runners around me—even the faster ones—who kept me going. Good leaders surround themselves with smarter, stronger people, all while recognizing that together we can reach further.

8. **Build sisterhood and healthy relationships:** Who is in your sisterhood? Building and nurturing your inner circle of trusted friends keeps you grounded, accountable and gives you the space to be yourself. Surround yourself with people who build you up, protect you and remind you that you are capable enough.

9. **Develop an expertise:** Let your passion motivate you to become an expert.

10. **Joy:** Don't underestimate the importance of having fun. Stress is problematic for individuals and organizations. When you find joy in the small things, you are able to foster gratitude, and strong leaders recognize that joy is essential to get us through trials.

HELGA FLORES TREJO

Helga Flores Trejo was born in Mexico (and chooses not to share her date of birth or further personal details). She earned her Master in Political Sciences, International Law and Latin America Studies at the Johann Wolfgang Goethe-Universitat Frankfurt in 1995. In 2020 she became the vice president for Global Public Affairs International Organizations at Bayer Global. She has held leadership positions in government, international organizations and the private sector. She broke barriers by becoming one of the few immigrant staffers in the German Parliament (1995-1998) and the first immigrant to lead a German foundation in Washington, DC: the Heinrich Böll Foundation North America (2003-2008). Flores Trejo is co-founder of the Latinos in Foreign Policy network, which provides fellowships and exchange programs for Latinos with multiple transatlantic organizations. She has served on the Board of Cultural Vistas as well as the National Committee of the Latino Victory Project.

cᔧᎦ ᎦᎦᎴ

Helga's Top 10 Leadership Lessons

1. **Take risks:** I genuinely believe that the greatest growth happens outside of your comfort zone. I have left my country (twice) and have left comfortable and relevant professional positions to take on new challenges. By and large, taking risks has proven rewarding; it also has allowed me to test myself, grow as a person and as a leader.

2. **Embrace change:** Change and ambiguity are the new normal. Many times, I have experienced change I was unable to influence; the uncertainty about the unknown is scary. But instead of trying to hold on to the past in vain, I have tried to embrace new opportunities that offer transformation and even rupture.

3. **Be curious:** The rapid transformation of our societies, the speed of innovation and the intensity of global competition require each of us to be always aware and open to continuous learning. Curiosity is an attribute I always look for in the people I supervise or work with, and it has served me personally very well.

4. **Ask for advice and, yes, even for help:** I strive to be strong and overcome any challenge on my own; hence I know very well that it is not easy to ask for help, because you feel you do not want to bother others. But I have learned over the years that most leaders are open and even glad to offer advice or help when possible.

5. **It all starts with empathy:** Never lose your ability to put yourself in somebody else's shoes, whether in negotiations, in sensitive diplomatic situations or in day-to-day engagement with your colleagues. You can best achieve great things when you start with empathy.

6. **Change places from the inside:** To be a changemaker you need to be willing to take responsibility and change institutions from the inside. Especially large institutions benefit from people who defy well-worn tracks—even if your boss won't always see it that way.

7. **Pursue an idea, not a position:** When I look back at my professional path, I can say that I always chose challenging tasks that I was passionate about and that would allow me to learn something new. It is in this space, where I want to spend my time and pour my efforts. So, pursue the task, not the position.

8. **Networking is not a dirty word:** Many times I have noticed that people refer to networking with certain loathing or, at the very least, with discomfort. But networking is about building meaningful relationships, about connecting to people's passions and interests to the benefit of all. Networking is not optional; it is an essential part of being an effective leader and a changemaker.

9. **Be a mentor and a mentee:** In every position I have held, I served as mentor and was a mentee both formally and informally. I have made a personal commitment to never pretend to be too busy for this kind of engagement. It has always been a learning experience and a joy and allowed me to grow professionally and as leader.

10. **"If you want to go quickly, go alone; if you want to go far, go together":** This is an African proverb I fully embrace. In such times of great transformation, uncertainty, growing inequality and imperfect justice, it is more important than ever to build and maintain a community and to promote common action.

SYLVIA R. GARCIA

Sylvia R. Garcia was born the eighth of ten children to native Texan parents on September 6, 1950, in San Diego, Texas. Garcia earned a scholarship to Texas Woman's University in Denton, where she graduated with a degree in Social Work and Political science in 1972. She then received her JD from the Thurgood Marshall School of Law at Texas Southern University in Houston in 1978. Garcia was elected to the US House of Representatives in November 2018, becoming the first Latina ever to represent Texas' 29th Congressional District. Prior to her political career, Garcia served as director and presiding judge of the Houston Municipal Court System for an unprecedented five terms under two mayors from 1987 to 1997. She was elected and served as city controller from 1998 to 2002 and then was elected to the Harris County Commissioners' Court and served from 2002 to 2010. She was the first Hispanic and first woman to ever be elected in her own right to that office. She was next elected to the Texas State Senate in 2013 and in 2019 to Congress, where she serves on the House Judiciary and House Financial Services committees. During her first year in Congress, she played a critical role in the impeach-ment investigation against President Donald J. Trump. On Janu-ary 15, 2020, she was selected as one of seven impeachment man-agers tasked with making the case to the American people and the Senate for the removal of Donald J. Trump as President of the United States. Among her awards are the Nancy Pelosi Award for Policy (2021); the Legislator of the Year, National Association for Bilingual Education (2021); the Working Families Champion Award, TX Gulf Coast Area Labor Federation (2017); and the Matt García Public Service Award, Mexican American Legal De-fense and Education Fund (2017).

ぐの ๑ఴ

Sylvia's Top 10 Leadership Lessons

1. **Believe in God, work hard, get educated:** My parents always taught me to work hard, get an education and believe in God. They also taught me we are all God's children, and it is up to us to advocate for a world where we are all treated as such. This is a lesson I often remember, one that has guided me through life.

2. **Show up and be on time:** My parents drilled in us to be on time, to look presentable and to be courteous, and to always follow the Golden Rule, especially if we expect others to show up for us.

3. **Take pride in yourself:** Never forget where you come from. Growing up, my mom always reminded me that no matter what I did in life, I had to always remember that I am a "Garcia."

4. **Put people first:** Always remember to extend a hand and give a hand to those who need help. My mother always said that no matter how poor we were, there was someone else poorer. That is why for me public service has always been about putting people first.

5. **Value hard work; it gets you to your goals:** Growing up picking cotton in rural South Texas, I learned firsthand about the value of hard work. I have never forgotten the time I spent in those cotton fields. Those moments remind me of the importance of working hard every day to achieve your goals.

6. **Be HIP when you get a seat at the table:** When you get a seat at the table, make sure you are part of the conversation. Speak up, interrupt if you have to and work to make sure others have a seat at the table too. I have also always focused on being "HIP": working with **h**onesty, **i**ntegrity and **p**rofessionalism. It really goes a long way.

7. *No te dejes/***Never give up; do better:** Failure is nothing but an obstacle. When you fail, pick yourself up, determine what you can do better and work harder to achieve your goals. Never give up.

8. **I have the power to create a country of equal justice:** As a trained lawyer, a former judge and an impeachment manager, I have learned about the importance of creating a country where everyone can get equal justice under the law and that no one is above it, not even the president.

9. **Be that experienced change agent:** As a former social worker, I saw how the most vulnerable among us can be failed by politics. I always try to put myself in someone else's shoes. It is why I bring the perspective of social work into my policy-making.

10. **Always reassess and recharge with fun:** Through all of your hard work, take time to have a little fun. Ask yourself, "Am I having fun?" because if you are not, you need to reassess or recharge.

ZANTÉ GARCÍA

Second-generation Mexican-American Zanté García was born on November 3, 1962, in Garden City, Kansas. She earned her Associate in Criminal Justice in 1987 from Garden City Community College and her BA in Sociology from the University of New Mexico in 1991. In 2006, García graduated with a Master in Bilingual Education from Southern Methodist University in Dallas, Texas. García works as a bilingual third-grade teacher in the Dallas Independent School District. She has been a leading early childhood educator, social activist, spiritual leader and board member of the Promise United Church of Christ. She has also fought for gender, racial and marriage equality for LGBTQ persons. García has served on the boards of Hope for Peace and Justice, a social activist nonprofit group, and The Walk Spiritual Retreat Community.

ↁ Ɽ

Zanté's Top 10 Leadership Lessons

1. **Be authentic:** Don't change who you are or give others the opportunity to tell you who you are. There is only one fabulous you.
2. **Be honest:** Truth will never catch you in a lie, even if it's uncomfortable.
3. **Give to others:** We're all here for a purpose. We all need one another. You won't lose out on anything by giving. It will all come back to you in abundance.
4. **Love yourself:** Don't be afraid to look at the "ugly" side of things. Walk straight into it, face it, embrace it and let it go. When you do this, loving others comes easy.
5. **Work hard:** Do a little extra if you have to. It's better to eat a little *caca* now than for the rest of your life.
6. **Forgive:** People make mistakes and do *pendejadas*. Let it go; not everyone is as magnificent as you are.
7. **Be humble:** Yes! You are fabulous, but to *Diosito* you're one of many.
8. **Laugh at your mistakes:** Learn from them and try again to do your best.
9. **Lead by example:** Don't expect others to meet your needs. Show them that you are a strong and confident *mujer*.
10. **Be thankful:** Love everything that you have: *familia, amistades, casa, comida, respiración, trabajo y salud*. Love being alive, no matter the circumstances, "God, never wastes a hurt."

GRACE ELENA GARNER

Grace Elena Garner was born on January 6, 1986, in Twenty-Nine Palms Marine Corps Base, California. She earned her BA in Political Studies and Gender Feminist Studies from Pitzer College in 2007 and her JD from California Western School of Law in 2013. A practicing attorney in the areas of employment and municipal law, she was elected to the Palm Springs City Council in 2019. Garner began her career in Washington, DC as a legislative assistant for women's issues for a progressive religious organization; she lobbied Congress for comprehensive sexuality education and LGBTQ equality, among other issues. Garner returned to her hometown and served as a member of the Palm Springs Planning Commission and the City Council.

∽◌ ◌∾

Grace's Top 10 Leadership Lessons

1. **Bring people in:** When you walk in a room, take a long look. Who is there? Who is not? Where are the voices that are missing? Take the time to get to know your community and bring in all of the voices you encounter.
2. **Be yourself:** Authenticity matters when connecting with others. Don't worry about what people want to hear; instead speak your truth. Share your views and what you learn from others because you believe in them, not because someone tells you it's what people want to hear.
3. **Honor your roots:** Our ancestors allowed us to arrive where we are today. Value their lessons, learn from their mistakes and take pride in their successes.
4. **Speak up:** Use your voice. Never take for granted what you bring to the discussion. Even the smallest idea can be the spark for something greater.
5. **Be patient:** Take a deep breath and count to five when needed.
6. **Listen to the community:** No one knows the needs of the community better than the community itself. Make sure the community is always part of the conversation.
7. **Remember why you started your journey:** Take the time to write down or video-record why you have chosen your path. What drives you? Share your why with others and use it to move you forward.
8. **Take care of yourself as you take care of others:** Your well-being is just as important as the work you do. To be successful you need to take care of yourself too.
9. **Encourage others:** Everyone has something to offer. Encourage others to get involved and achieve their goals.
10. **Read, read, read:** Take advantage of your local library. Read a vast array of works. Reading can be your escape, your inspiration, your success and so much more.

LETITIA "LETI" GÓMEZ

Letitia Gómez was born September 26, 1954, in San Antonio, Texas. She earned a degree in General Studies from San Antonio College in 1975, a BA in Sociology from the University of Texas in 1977 and Master in Urban Studies at Trinity University in 1987. In her thirty-three-year federal career, she has risen to her present position of GS-15 Asset Management Business Line Leader. After some experience in organizing with the Texas Farm Workers in 1977 she began organizing with the Gay Chicano Caucus in Houston and later helped plan the first Texas Latina Lesbian retreat and organize the Gay and Lesbian Tejano Network. In 1987 she was founding co-chair of the first national Latina/o LGBT organization, LLEGO. Gómez served as its executive director from 1993 to 1995. During the 1990s, she also served as president of ENLACE, a social support organization for lesbian and gay Latinas/os in the DC metro area, participated in organizing the 1991 National Lesbian Conference, served on DC's Civilian Complaint Review Board and on the boards of DC Council on Women and AIDs, the National Lesbian and Gay

Health Foundation, the AIDs Action, the DC Latino Civil Rights Taskforce and the DC Democratic State Committee. Over the years and to the present, she has maintained this level of involvement and leadership. Among her numerous awards are the League of United Latin American Citizens Woman of the Year Award (2019), the Latino GLBT History Project Mujer en el Movimiento Award (2013), the Meritorious Civilian Service Award from the US Department of the Navy (2003), the Plumed Warrior Award Premio Mujer (2001) and the Distinguished Service Award of the Gay and Lesbian Activist Alliance (1993).

❦ ❦

Leti's Top 10 Leadership Lessons

1. **Show that you care for people:** Especially, the people you lead and rely on.
2. **Listen:** I work at being a good listener and hearing people. I've gotten feedback that doing this is appreciated.
3. **Be open to opinions and ideas different from yours:** You might find a better one.
4. **Trust:** Trust your intelligence and that of others.
5. **Make your voice heard:** You may have to raise your voice and repeat, especially when the majority in the room are men.
6. **Encourage women to challenge themselves to lead:** Be ready to support their leadership.
7. **Defend the rights of people in the workplace and community:** Interrupt the oppression and be aware of your own biases.
8. **Challenge yourself to try things that you haven't done before:** You will always learn from the experience.
9. **Build a network of support for yourself:** It can be lonely in leadership positions, especially if you lead an organization. Your network will listen to you, give you feedback and be a shoulder to cry on if needed.
10. **Appreciate yourself:** You have achieved a leadership position. You know what it took to get to here.

BARBARA GÓMEZ-AGUIÑAGA

Barbara Gómez-Aguiñaga was born on March 6, 1992, in Lagos de Moreno, Jalisco, Mexico and moved to the United States in August 2010. Today, she is a professor of public policy and social equity in the School of Public Administration at the University of Nebraska, Omaha. Dr. Gómez-Aguiñaga has served as an independent research contractor for the American Civil Liberties Union (ACLU) of New Mexico, conducting research on the use of solitary confinement across the state. She also served as a research assistant in the Migration Policy Institute in Washington, DC, providing support for the US Immigration Policy Program on issues such as immigration enforcement and deferred action. She served in a similar capacity in the Immigrant Legal Resource Center in San Francisco, CA, where she worked on immigration enforcement policies, unaccompanied minors and the DACA program. She also conducted field work in southern and western Mexico to study migration from Mexico and Central America to the United States for the Cross Border Issues Group and was a Research Consultant to Latino Decisions from 2017 to 2020.

Some of her notable awards include the Scholars Strategy Network and the Robert Wood Johnson Foundation's Health Equity Scholar in 2021; the Association for Education in Journalism and Mass Communication's Nafziger-White-Salwen Dissertation Award; Runner-up in 2021 and Best Research Paper Award for the Race, Ethnicity and Politics Section of the American Political Science Association in 2020. Her research has been featured in *The New York Times* and NBC News. Her work has led to policy changes in the criminal justice system of New Mexico; she has been cited in US courts, the US Senate and Congress, especially on addressing the incorporation of immigrant youth. She earned her PhD in Political Science at the University of New Mexico in May 2020, conducting applied and academic research in racial inequalities in public policy, Latina/o/x politics and race and ethnicity.

⸙ ⸙

Barbara's Top 10 Leadership Lessons

1. **Embrace what makes you different:** One of my biggest insecurities when I moved to the United States was that I didn't look or sound like most Americans. I used to think that if I were just like everyone else, my life would be better, but you guessed it: I was wrong! What makes you different is what makes you powerful. You're unique, and nobody will ever be like you; embrace it and enjoy it.

2. **Apply, apply, apply!** Something I've learned over the years is that you have to apply for that scholarship, award, job or internship. If you don't, somebody else will do it and they will get it, even with fewer qualifications, less passion or commitment. Research shows that most women feel like they have to meet 100% of the criteria to apply for jobs, whereas men do it with about 60%. Break that tendency and apply for whatever you're interested in. Pro-tip: self-nominate for awards (Yes, it's totally fine. I've done it and it works!).

3. **Don't be afraid of rejection:** I can't tell you how much I've learned and gained from rejections. Yes, rejections seem intimidating and can be emotionally tolling in the beginning, but they will take you one step closer to your next acceptance. The more rejections you receive, the easier it becomes and the more likely you are to get acceptances along the way.

4. **Learn to say no:** We live in an era when everyone is expected to be hyper productive and have tons of personal connections (look at how many friends you have on Facebook!). But you are allowed to say "no." Besides being a sign of respect, saying no can set you free for better relationships and things that are truly important to you.

5. **Know your talents:** All of us are worthy, and we are also good at something not just professionally but also personally. Are you good at writing, public speaking, organizing, cooking, following deadlines, listening, being supportive, memorizing, being caring, volunteering, being considerate, etc.? Identify and acknowledge your talents and put them into practice!

6. **Tell others about their talents:** While self-reflection may be hard, it is way easier to identify somebody else's talents. Don't stop there . . . tell them what you think they are good at! Not only is it kind, but it can also make a tremendous difference in their lives. I, for example, would not be an academic if my advisor hadn't told me that I was good at research.

7. **Ask for help:** You don't need to reinvent the wheel when you're lost. There are several folks and resources out there that can be tremendously helpful and useful when you have questions or concerns about professional or personal matters. Sometimes the answer to your questions is an email or a book away.

8. **Dare to try something new:** One of the best ways to find yourself is by trying new things. Whether it is food, sports, careers or cities. Trying something new will help you grow and know yourself better. Worst case, you get to learn what you don't like (which is also a valuable lesson!).

9. **Take care of your health:** It does not matter who you are: Health is the most precious gift one can have. Without health, you have nothing. So please take care of yourself both physically and mentally because nobody else can do it for you.

10. **Pay it forward:** While Latinas, women of color, first-generation college students and immigrants are underrepresented in many spaces, we have to acknowledge and be grateful for the brave, strong and courageous women who have paved the way for us. Not only that, but we have to be actively committed to continue the fight for ourselves, our communities and future generations.

FRANKIE GONZALES-WOLFE

Frankie Gonzales-Wolfe is a small business owner and serves as the owner/CEO of MG Parking Systems. Additionally, Frankie serves as the chief of staff to Bexar County Commissioner Rebeca Clay-Flores. In 2019, she ran for the San Antonio City Council; as such, she would have been the first openly transgender elected official in Texas. For the past 24 years, Gonzales-Wolfe has held two careers that have run congruently with each other: one in the financial services industry and the other in San Antonio's largest companies servicing the military community. At a Fortune 500 company, she managed teams in retail banking, risk mitigation, organizational development and human resources. In her political career, she has participated in local, state and national campaigns as an intern, organizer, campaign strategist/consultant and campaign manager.

❦

Frankie's Top 10 Leadership Lessons

1. **Kick up some dirt:** If you want to change the landscape, you must kick up a little dirt.
2. **Representation matters**: Don't ever be afraid of bringing your own chair to the table when someone refuses to provide you a seat.
3. **Decisions have consequences:** No matter what decision you make, there will always be a consequence. Consequences don't always mean something negative. Always be prepared for what may come.
4. **Don't take politics personal:** We all have a difference of opinion and won't always agree on policy or thoughts. But having mutual respect for one another is key to compromise.
5. **Live your truth:** We have only one life to live. So, live it knowing your value and worth, and don't let others dictate your success.
6. **Give it back as freely as you got it:** Mentors in our lives taught us what we know. It's our obligation to teach the next generation of leaders to continue the fight.
7. **Lead with empathy:** Don't look down on others unless you are reaching down to lift them up. See the world through their eyes and keep an open mind to learn.
8. **Do what's right even when no one is watching**: You can't be motivated by a spotlight; you have to be motivated with the satisfaction that you did the right thing.
9. **Mistakes don't define you**: If you make a mistake, ensure that the mistake taught you a valuable lesson. Lessons provide us an opportunity to grow.
10. **Listen more and talk less**: A leader listens and absorbs feedback. That is how smart decisions are made.

ELIZABETH R. GUZMÁN

Elizabeth R. Guzmán was born on February 13, 1973, in Lima, Perú, and immigrated to the United States as a single mother who put herself through community college, juggling three jobs to pay for a one-bedroom apartment. She obtained her associate degree from Northern Virginia Community College in 2003, a BA in Public Safety from Capella University in 2011 and a Master in Social Work from the University of Southern California in August 2016; she also obtained a Master in Public Administration from American University in 2013. She is a social worker in the Alexandria Department of Community and Human Services; in 2017, she became the first Hispanic immigrant woman ever elected to the Virginia House of Delegates. In 2018, Guzmán delivered the Spanish-language response to the State of the Union address. As a delegate, she has been a leader in the area of juvenile justice reform and fought for three years to successfully pass legislation to raise the age at which children can be tried as adults. Guzmán currently serves on the Virginia Commission on Youth, the State Executive Council for Children's Services and the

Prince William County Jail Board. She is also vice president of AFSCME Local 3001, a member of the National Latina State Legislative Caucus of the Board of Latino Legislative Leaders, the Southeast Region chair for the National Hispanic Caucus of State Legislators, the political director for the Democratic Latinos of Virginia, among many other leadership positions. Her awards include the Highest Honor Friend of Education from the Virginia Education Association (2021), the Legislative Leader Award from the League of Conservation Voters (2020), the Legislator of the Year from the Virginia Education Association (2020), the Legislative Champion from the Sierra Club (2019) and the NOVA Labor Legislative Champion (2018).

cᒥᔕ ᕮᑐᕳ

Elizabeth's Top 10 Leadership Lessons

1. **Be persistent:** Nothing has been easy for us. Fight for what you believe is right. Stand up and speak out when your heart is telling you to do it.
2. **Be strong:** Your life experiences have shown you that everything that happened in your life had a reason. Even when it hurts, always think about the future. Pain is temporary, and there is always a lesson learned to prepare you for a better future.
3. **Be accessible:** Remember how many people did not answer the phone or did not care about you or your ideas? Creating a pipeline of future Latina leaders is going to depend on your accessibility to share your life experiences to future generations.
4. **Don't allow anyone to define you:** You represent yourself and you are allowed to describe the best version of you with strengths and weaknesses, with pros and cons. Your story belongs only to you, and you can make the best out of it.
5. **Be an active member in your community:** You never know when you are going to inspire a new Latinx individual to do something better or bigger. They need to see you, so they know that there is someone out there who looks like them who is a leader and so they can believe it is possible for them too.
6. **Be proactive and don't procrastinate:** Take your time to be prepared because we always have to prove ourselves. Don't wait for information to come to you. Go and get it. It is great to be the first, but you don't want to be the last, so being the first means leaving a good impression.

7. **Representation matters:** Our children's future in this country depends on us. We do not want our children to be less of an American because they are brown or their last name is Guzmán, García, etc. Fighting for a better future means having a voice at the table. Empower other Latinas to do what you are doing.

8. **Don't be complacent:** Challenge yourself and challenge the status quo. Having a better future means being comfortable with change. You can lead that change by setting an example.

9. **Smile even in difficult times:** Things will not always go your way. However, no one needs to know that. Smiling even when someone is attacking you will show who the bigger person is. Breathe deeply and keep going.

10. **Be authentic:** Don't pretend to be someone else. You are unique. God created you that way. Show your true self and you will inspire others.

KARELIA HARDING

Karelia Harding was born on June 9, 1971, in Tegucigalpa, Honduras. She immigrated from Honduras on August 2, 1995, and became an US citizen on March 19, 2008. Harding received her bachelor's and master's degrees in Education while in Honduras and began her career as a teacher there. She is currently the Parent Engagement and Equity Manager at the Oregon Child Development Coalition (OCDC) since 2002. The OCDC is the third largest Migrant and Seasonal Head Start Program in the United States; it also serves regular Head Start programs. Prior to working with Head Start in 2002, she was a pre-school teacher (1994-1996), an assistant director and later program director for Camp Fire Boys (1996-2002) in Portland. Harding serves on the boards of the National Migrant and Seasonal Head Start Association, the National Head Start Association, the Equity Advisory Committee for Education, the National Migrant and Seasonal Head Start Collaboration Advisory Council and the Oregon Migrant Education State Parent Advisory Committee. Harding's most notable awards include the National Migrant Seasonal Head Start Association Appreciation Award in 2014, the Harvest of Hope Award in 2004 and the Multnomah County Volunteer Award in 2000.

৻৶৹ ৻৸৹

Karelia's Top 10 Leadership Lessons

1. **Don't think outside the box; explode the box:** Do not let any-one put your thoughts or directions in a box; neither should you ever put anyone's in a box. Once you see that the box does not exist, you will see things from new perspectives.
2. **Stay true to yourself and be proud:** Be honest and do not change who you are or your values because of certain cir-cumstances or other people's desires and opinions. Credible leaders practice what they preach. Your credibility and values are the foundation of who you are as a leader.
3. **Recognize your strengths and weaknesses:** Do not be afraid of them, embrace them; that is what makes you unique and different from others. Weaknesses are areas in need of im-provement; do not see them as negative.
4. **Recognize and trust your team:** Every person brings different values, ideas and perspectives to the table. Allow others to lead; you don't have to be always at the front. Help them grow, even if that means losing them, and recognize their value and what they bring to the table.
5. **Maintain a good sense of humor:** Maintain your sense of humor, even in problematic situations, and look for the bright side in everything. Your team will mirror your feelings. It is okay to step away from the problem, have a good laugh and get back to work.
6. **Be a visionary by thinking of the impact:** Often it is hard to imagine how things will take place or work out. Through ac-knowledging the effect/impact by thinking through each de-cision, it will provide you with a better outcome.

7. **It is not about how we fail; it is about how we get back up after we've failed:** Don't be afraid; everyone has failed at some time in their life. Failures or challenges help us to be better. Be strong and get up, clean your clothes, lift up your chin, keep going, don't stop.

8. **Be a mentor but become a mentee:** Surround yourself with people whom you admire and who inspire you. They will challenge you, but always be ready to give back to others, build into the next generation. Always think about the future and the impact you will have on future leaders. Be a mentor.

9. **Be open and caring towards others:** This is about putting yourself in someone else's shoes. If you are available to others and show you care, you will get people on your team that will support you to the end.

10. **Take time for you, learn to say no:** Make sure to take time for what makes you grounded and do not compromise this time. In my case, this is family. Make sure to make time to do something you love and do it even when you feel there is no time. Remember to balance your time because if you put all your time in your work, you are taking time from the ones you love or the things that make you grounded.

LINA HIDALGO

Lina Hidalgo was born on February 19, 1991, in Bogotá, Columbia, and moved to Houston, Texas in 2005. She became a naturalized citizen in 2013. She received her degree in Political Science from Stanford University in 2013. Hidalgo is the first woman to be elected county judge (in 2019), the presiding administrator over the Harris County governing body; Harris County is the most populous county in Texas and the third largest county in our nation. She was the youngest, at age twenty-eight, ever elected to that position. Today, she is the most popular politician in the county, having successfully led the residents through hurricanes, floods and the COVID pandemic. She has received numerous awards, including the John F. Kennedy New Frontier Award, Jack Brooks Foundation Leadership Award, *Time Magazine* the 100 Next and *Forbes'* 30 Under 30.

ᥫᩙ ᥏᮪

Lina's Top 10 Leadership Lessons

1. **Challenge the status quo:** Never decide something can't be done because it has never been done before. Whenever someone tells me about the way something has to be, the way it's always been done, my response is usually, "Why?"
2. **Don't ask for permission to make your voice heard:** Participation matters. When you ask people to participate, they show up. Folks want to help improve their communities if you give them a chance.
3. **Work with a sense of urgency:** It's okay to be in a hurry to get things done. Your only limit is your own imagination.
4. **Take care of yourself:** You're only as strong as your own ability to stay resilient.
5. **Act courageously:** Never seize to act out of fear of failure. Leadership requires making bold decisions. Sometimes "playing it safe" just isn't enough.
6. **Empower others:** We can't do this alone. Let's lift each other up to achieve our common goals.
7. **Be the change:** Change starts small. If we all do our part to be the change we're working towards, together, we can make it a reality.
8. **Remain connected, remain present:** Don't forget about the "why." Continue to empathize with those you serve.
9. **Exude kindness:** Not only with those who agree with you and share your vision but also with those who may doubt you. It can truly go a long way.
10. **Trust your moral compass:** It's much easier to make decisions when you know what's right.

MICHELLE N. KIDANI

Michelle N. Kidani was born on September 30, 1948, in Honolulu, Hawaii, to a Japanese American father and Puerto Rican mother. She received her BS in Business Administration in 1993 from Kennedy-Western University (now Warren National University). Kidani has served in the Hawaii State Senate as the senate vice president since 2017, having first been elected to that body in 2008. Nationally, she is a member of the Board of Hispanic Caucus Chairs and the National Latina State Legislative Caucus. She is vice president and current director of the Mililani Town Association, the largest homeowner's association in the state. Among her awards are the Adult Friends for Youth PEARL Hero Award (2021), Hawaii Association of Behavior Analysis Community Contribution Award (2018), the Legislator of the Year by the Hawaii Dental Association (2018), the National Conference Co-Chair Appreciation Award of the Board of Hispanic Caucus Conference (2013) and the Hawaii Women's Political Caucus.

⟟⟒

Michelle's Top 10 Leadership Lessons

1. **Be a teacher and a mentor, not just a boss:** Give advice and feedback, delegate projects, show you care. Help your workers and mentees find better opportunities.
2. **Collaborate often to build alliances:** Gain cooperation through teamwork to reach your goals.
3. **Be a good listener:** Listen carefully before you speak. Listen more than you speak. Ask good questions. Make eye contact with the person speaking.
4. **Communicate:** Speak clearly in words that all understand. Don't humiliate or embarrass others—it doesn't make you look superior.
5. **Promotion opportunities:** Always look for promotion opportunities for your staff, even when you think they are irreplaceable, even when it means they will leave your employ.
6. **Delegate:** We can't be everything to everyone. We can't be in more than one place at one time. It's okay to let others take the lead to get the job done.
7. **Team building:** Help the creativity. Encourage others to share ideas through brainstorming. Connect with others who want to collaborate.
8. **Motivate:** It's difficult to lead if you are not willing to also follow. Show others you are the person you want them to be.
9. **Accountability and flexibility:** The buck stops here. Own your mistakes. Know when to change course or change team members or when to admit a task is not possible with new obstacles or limitations.
10. **Integrity:** To me, this means being a professional human being. Being ethical, being reliable and being honest.

DIANA MALDONADO

Diana Maldonado was born on January 22, 1963, in Lubbock, Texas. She received her BS in Business Administration from St. Edward's University in 2000. She currently serves as president and CEO of the Greater Austin Hispanic Chamber of Commerce. She was the first Latina elected to represent Williamson County in the Texas House of Representatives and served from 2009 to 2011. Prior to that, she served six years on the Round Rock ISD Board of Trustees (2003-2008) and as its president. While in public service, she also worked as a financial advisor in the private sector (2013-2020). She continues to serve on education and leadership boards as president for Seedling Mentors, the Advisory Council for The Bill Munday School of Business at St. Edward's University and the National Association of Latino Elected Officials. Included among her awards are the First Tee Greater Austin Philanthropic Leadership Award (2021), the Finalist Austin Business Journal Profiles in Power (2021), Freshman of the Year of the Legislative Study Group (2009) and the Texas State Comptroller's Personal & Professional Development Award (1999).

ఆఁ ఁ

Diana's Top 10 Leadership Lessons

1. **Keep it simple:** In life, whether it's work or some important facet in your life, we tend to overthink, over rationalize that we miss the lesson and opportunity. Declutter your mind to bring the powerful thoughts to the forefront. Declutter your home to bring positive energy to your space. These are some examples that have catapulted me to where I want to go.

2. **Lead with grace:** Be prepared and put your best foot forward because even if you fall, you will own every step of the way!

3. **Be in the moment:** In today's world, there's the instant gratification and the sky is falling syndromes, and we find ourselves taking calls, texting while we are with someone else, making them wait. Take the time to be with that person; more times than not, the call and text can wait.

4. **Enjoy the quiet time:** Stillness, being alone with your thoughts allows for you to center, breathe and acknowledge yourself. I enjoy this especially in the early morning, meditating, walking or running.

5. **Never stop learning:** Reading is a pastime favorite I recently rediscovered, and it's amazing how reading opens your brain waves and deepens your knowledge rather than surface level talk.

6. **Say thank you:** To yourself for all the hard work you do for others. And it also helps to say it to others. It'll make for a better place.

7. **Take care of your health:** Mind, body, soul. It won't help if you're the smartest, richest or notable person, if you don't integrate a regimen of health in working out, eating well and enriching your spirit.

8. **There are possibilities beyond your horizon:** Think big and dream boldly. Have affirmations all around and believe them. They DO happen!

9. **Pay it forward:** The gift of sharing. Help others connect to the pieces quicker by sharing insights, experiences and making yourself available to those who want to grow and learn. The things I've learned that someone shared with me, I in turn want to pay them forward.

10. **Find your voice:** Thoughts, words, actions. Speak your truth because there is only one you! We oftentimes are afraid to say something wrong. I wrongly doubted myself early on. In the times we live in now, people want our voices, and there are many issues that beg for our voices to tell stories and perspectives. Voice it with a smile!

ANNABEL MANCILLAS

Annabel Mancillas was born on February 19, 1983, in Hutchinson, Kansas, to Mexican immigrant parents. She earned an Associate in Nursing from Hutchinson Community College and her BS in Nursing and in Arts Premedicine from Wichita State University. She went on to earn a Master in Public Health in 2021 and a Doctor of Medicine degree in 2011 both from the University of Kansas School of Medicine. Mancillas, MD, MPH serves as an assistant clinical professor in the Department of OB/Gyn at the University of Kansas Medical Center and is an attending clinical faculty member of The University of Kansas Health System. Dr. Mancillas has dedicated her life to serving her community and providing healthcare in her community. At the age of 17, Mancillas started volunteering as a Spanish-English interpreter at the health department in her hometown of Hutchinson, where her desire to provide healthcare was solidified. She became a certified nurse's aide and started working at the local hospital, then went to higher education. Mancillas was selected as a fellow of the American College of Obstetrics and Gynecology in 2018 and became board certified in Obstetrics and Gynecology in 2017.

ໆ⊚ ⊚ᨆ

Annabel's Top 10 Leadership Lessons

1. ***Ponte las pilas*. Literally translates to "Put in your batteries":** It was a common phrase my Mexican parents would tell me as a child if I was slow to do something or showed lack of motivation. They continued to tell me this as a high schooler, in undergrad and in medical school. Instead of my initial perceived interpretation of "hurry up" or "get moving," this phrase turned into their endearing "Don't give up", "Keep going" or simply *"Ponte las pilas."*

2. **Work hard:** I have read a saying that being a daughter of an immigrant you were "born to hustle, raised humbly and taught to value life's blessing." BORN TO HUSTLE. You can't expect to succeed at anything without putting in the work that's required.

3. **Respect those around you:** Being a certified nurse's aide, interpreter, registered nurse and now physician EVERY SINGLE role has taught me invaluable lessons . . . most of all how to treat others with respect and that prestigious letters behind your name mean nothing if you do not respect the people around you.

4. **Have a loyal network of friends—quality, not quantity:** This is not to be confused with networking; your network should stretch far and wide. But I'm referring to those you trust with your all, your confidants, the people who you allow to see the tears. My journey has many success stories, but also behind those stories are the struggles to get there. My sister, my best friends since sixth grade, my best friends from medical school, my best friend from residency, my sorority sisters, close colleagues and my husband, have seen my tears, and I have also seen their tears and stood by them in their journeys.

5. **Have short-term and long-term goals:** Keep your eye on the prize and make a plan to get there. There will be setbacks. There will be times when you think it's unattainable but remind yourself of your goals and review your plans of how you will get there. This will help you refocus and direct you back on track.

6. **Love yourself:** Learn to love yourself. Accept who you are. Accept what you look like. Don't be ashamed of who you are, where you're from and how you got here. You cannot be a good leader if you do not love yourself.

7. **Balance:** I will tell you that this is still a difficult one for me as a physician, a wife and a mom. You cannot be a leader if you are overextended. Find your professional passions and make time for them; know your personal passions and make time for them. But always remember to make time for yourself. You can't starve a dairy cow and expect milk.

8. **Know your worth:** Professionally and personally. You worked hard to be where you are; make sure you are being compensated for all the assets you bring to the table. Do not be afraid to negotiate for what you deserve. Do not be afraid to leave if you are not valued.

9. **Surround yourself with the positive:** Positive friends, people, activities. This energy helps keep you on track, especially when you feel yourself getting off track.

10. **Ask for help.** Know your limitations. Never be scared but especially never be too proud to ask for help. Do what you can first. Don't expect anyone to do your work for you but know when you need help and ask for it.

LIDIA S. MARTINEZ

Lidia S. Martinez was born on May 18, 1962, in Ciudad Juárez Francisco Sarabia, Chihuahua, Mexico, and raised in El Paso, Texas. She came to the United States at the age of twelve in 1974 and became a naturalized citizen in 1989. Lidia received her degree in Business Administration with a focus in Marketing from the University of Texas at Arlington in 1989. Martínez retired as manager of Community Outreach for Southwest Airlines in 2020 after serving the airline for thirty years, ensuring that Southwest Airlines maintained a visible leadership position within the communities they served. She set the standard for outreach and corporate social responsibility. Martínez currently serves on the boards of the San Diego Regional Chamber of Commerce, The Campanile Foundation (San Diego State University) and the University of California San Diego Chancellor's Community Advisory Board, among others. Her awards include the San Diego Regional Chamber of Commerce Award Herb Klein Lifetime Achievement Award (2021), the San Diego Business Journal

Lifetime Achievement Award (2020), the Labor Council of Latin American Advancement Friend of LCLAA Award (2017), the Women's Advocate of the Year Women of Influence Awards (2016) and the California Rural Legal Assistance Dolores Huerta Award (2013).

ɔ@ ᖇɔ

Lidia's Top 10 Leadership Lessons

1. **Be a champion:** Advocate for those who are not or cannot be at the table. Help them be at the table by connecting them to the right people or opening doors they can't open on their own.
2. **Create strong collaborative relationships:** I have found that when you work with diverse people (age, color, gender, industry, etc.) who share your values and commitment to progress, you can more easily bring about sustainable change. But we must all come in with all our heart and soul for collaboration to have true impact.
3. **Be a mentor:** Your experience, wisdom and awareness can help others navigate through difficult situations and help them succeed. Don't be afraid to give tough love and hold them accountable. Don't waste your time with people who don't share your values or fail to pay it forward.
4. **Diversify your network:** I have benefitted a great deal from the support of people outside my comfortable circle of friends, outside my industry and outside my Latino community. I learned early in my career that I stood to learn a lot from those who did not look or think like me. Engaging in these diverse circles has also benefitted my community and people I love.
5. **Do the right thing, even when no one is watching:** Doing the right thing can often be challenging and can quickly multiply your critics, but that's the responsibility that comes with being a leader with integrity. Even when no one is watching, they are!

6. **Build bridges:** This has been great fun to do. It is so rewarding to see the positive outcomes that come from helping people build the foundation for strong relationships. I have faith in the links among all things. I believe there are few coincidences and that almost every connection has meaning.

7. **Find your superpower:** My superpower is my community. They have my back, and they keep me accountable and grounded. They give me the tough love my mother would give me. They also lift me and give me the confidence to continue advocating for them.

8. **Say I'm sorry only when you mean it:** We tend to be so apologetic, and "I'm sorry" comes easy to many of us. Practice saying it out loud ONLY when you mean it. Make note of how often you apologize and try to identify other words to use instead. If you have this awareness, you will also see that confident women rarely use it, and when they do, it is meaningful.

9. **Have fun. Why not?!:** Build a relaxed and fun culture around you and you will see how much more you can accomplish and how many more people will want to be around you. I have come across some very smart people who hardly ever smiled or took time to relax. I dreaded their company!

10. **Be your best advocate:** Learn your story and share it! Be proud of your accomplishments and don't shy away from asking for that promotion, that raise, that board seat, that spotlight that will help you help others. Ask people of influence, authority and power to champion you.

PATRICIA MEJIA

Patricia Mejia was born on May 1, 1979, in Corpus Christi, Texas. She has completed the Executive Leadership Program at Harvard and is a dual graduate of the BA and MA in Political Science from St. Mary's University in 2003. She has served as vice president for Community Engagement and Impact at the San Antonio Area Foundation since 2018. Mejia has twenty years of nonprofit and philanthropic leadership at such organizations as Methodist Healthcare Ministries (2014-2018), the National Association for Latino Community Asset Builders (2007-2012) and the 21st Century Leadership Center at St. Mary's University (2001-2007).

e❦ ❦v

Patricia's Top 10 Leadership Lessons

1. **Leadership "experts"** *no tienen nada* **on my** *mamá*: There is a ton of power in connecting to your roots, your first teachers; they may not have had the academic language but their lessons of navigating a world that was not made for them is exactly what you need to lead change.
2. *Dime con quién andas y te diré quién eres*: Tell me with whom you hang, and I will tell you who you are . . . that includes mentors. Dream of who you want to be and where you want to be, then build a network of mentors to support your growth and to honestly challenge you to grow.
3. **Channel your inner** *comadre*: Know how to build and sustain a relationship. Create a sense of brotherhood/sisterhood within your circle of influence by sharing resources and connections to support their growth. Share your story to connect with their stories.
4. **You can't always change hearts but jump at the opportunity to change policy/the rules:** We already know most policy/rules were not created to benefit all. Therefore, use your leadership to change any and all you can get your hands on to be more inclusive of your community. Leave the conversion of the hearts to the Creator.
5. **Use the present to create the future:** Time literally flies, whether you are working towards a better world or eating an *empanada*. This being true, dream what legacy you want to leave and use today to work towards that legacy. You won't see your fruit right away, but you will see it soon!
6. **Never be embarrassed to lay out the facts:** Tell funders, legislators the truth. Lay out the facts to demand what our community deserves, whether access to capital or simply to be at the table. It will likely make people uncomfortable, but that is what it takes to lead change.

7. **Trust your skillset! Walk in, rooted in your turquoise and gold hoops or wearing pearls, *si quieres*:** Allow yourself to be authentically you, owning your family's powerful history and knowing that it is unique and adds value. You deserve to be at the table—*con hoops y todo!*

8. **Remember that people are real and care about what matters to them, NOT what you think they should care about:** Work to understand their passion with intense listening and use that to connect to the agenda you are pushing. Be persistent and compassionate, all in one single move.

9. **Have conversations with people who do not agree with you:** You must understand the other side. Listen deeply, with compassion. You may never understand their logic (there may be none) but you will learn how to lay out your cards to stay in the game and possibly win.

10. **Use your life to fulfill the *promesas* your *mamá/abuela* made:** You and I are part of the most privileged generation, and we are rooted in the long line of strong women who came before us, struggled and literally made *promesas* to their creator so that you and I could be in "The room where it happens." Make it happen! A leader is a person engaged in a process of enabling and empowering others to accomplish shared objectives for the purpose of serving and benefiting the common good.

GLORIA MOLINA

Gloria Molina was born on May 31, 1948, in Montebello, California. Gloria attended East Los Angeles Community College and
California State University Los Angeles, part time from 1966 to
1974. Molina retired in 2014 after serving forty-three years in
elected public office, including as the Los Angeles County Supervisor of the First District where she served for more than two
decades. She is the founder of East Los Angeles' Comisión Fe-
menil Mexicana Nacional, a feminist organization and the
founder of La Plaza de Cultura y Artes, a museum dedicated to
the contributions of Latinos/as to the building of Los Angeles and
California. She started as a legal assistant to a state assembly-
man, then she served as deputy director of Presidential Personnel
in the Carter White House. In 1982, Gloria became the first
Latina to be elected to the California State Assembly. In 1991,
she was the first Latina elected to the Los Angeles County Board
of Supervisors. Molina was named as one of the Democratic
Party's "10 Rising Stars" by *Time Magazine* in 1996, and she
served as one of four vice chairs of the Democratic National

Committee through 2004. She currently serves as vice chair of the California Community Foundation and is a member of the Mexican American Legal and Defense Education Fund Board. She has received numerous awards for her public service, including the Águila Azteca from the president of Mexico. She received an Honorary Doctorate from Whittier College in 2012.

ເ✆ ૭ಿ

Gloria's Top 10 Leadership Lessons

1. **Honesty:** You must be honest with yourself and those who follow your leadership. There is a bond of trust developed between you and those who follow. It must be honored!
2. **Respect:** A leader must respect the role. In order to provide leadership to people, you must respect who they are, their values, culture and customs.
3. **Duty:** Leadership is a duty—you cannot just wear leadership. It is who you are. You must understand the duties and the seriousness associated with the role of leader.
4. *Ganas*/**Hard work:** Leadership requires hard work. You need to be abreast of issues; you must continue to read, research, investigate and recognize the *ganas* it takes to lead.
5. **Lead by example:** It is very important that a leader sets the example. No task is insignificant. You need to work shoulder to shoulder with people. Never ever think a job is too small for you.
6. **Protect your image:** The reason this is important is that folks rely on you. Corruption, scandal, lying will destroy the trust so essential to leadership.
7. **Passion and compassion:** Lead with passion and compassion. Be bold, be courageous and be strong. Passion must enter into every decision. Carry out your role with sincere compassion.
8. **Listen and accept criticism:** Leaders think they know it all and know best. Be a humble leader and listen to people. While we all hate to be criticized, do not let it consume you but accept and learn from it.
9. **Persistence:** Recognize that leadership does not get you to goals, but with passionate persistence—truly believing in your values and goals—your goals will be met.

10. **Self-care:** Leaders are warriors. Even the Aztecs sent their warriors to rest and reflect during battle. We need to step back from our leadership duty from time to time and take care of ourselves. Take days off, refresh yourself with family, get a massage, a pedicure or go shopping. Stop and smell las *rosas*!

M. LUCERO ORTIZ

M. Lucero Ortiz was born on November 13, 1979, in Orange, California, to Mexican immigrant parents. She earned a BA from the University of California, Los Angeles in 2004 and a law degree from the American University Washington College of Law in 2007. In addition, she earned her certificate in Non-Profit Executive Management at Georgetown University in 2018 and a certificate in Diversity, Equity and Inclusion in the Workplace from the University of South Florida in 2021. Lucero Ortiz works as an immigration attorney and human rights champion with over two decades of experience as a public policy advocate for workers' and immigrants' rights. She has also worked to enforce fair labor and occupational safety and health laws. Currently, Lucero Ortiz is the deputy director of Kids in Need of Defense. Previously, she served as the legal director at the Central American Resource Center (2018-2020), has been a political appointee at the US Department of Labor (2010-2014) and has also held positions at the Hispanic National Bar Association, the Congressional Hispanic Caucus Institute and the Mexican American

Legal Defense and Educational Fund. Lucero Ortiz has served on the board of the Hispanic Bar Association of the District of Columbia and Mary's Center. Among her numerous awards are the District of Columbia Mayor's Community Leadership Award for Immigration Justice (2019), the US Department of Labor Secretary's Exceptional Achievement Award (2012) and recognitions from the California State Legislature Assembly and City of Los Angeles.

ᥭ᠗ ᠗ᥩ

Lucero's Top 10 Leadership Lessons

1. **Celebrate diversity as a strength:** Among colleagues, the community and the world.
2. **Build self-care and mental health:** Even into the office culture, and it will help nurture solidarity and teamwork.
3. **Lead by example:** Model the commitment and self-care expected from team/colleagues.
4. **Connect mission and purpose:** To broader community, national and global causes.
5. **Embrace failure:** Build a culture of trial and error and innovation.
6. **Focus on strengths:** Rather than areas of improvement.
7. **Be a lifelong learner:** Admit mistakes and willingness to learn a new area.
8. **Always show appreciation:** Lead with gratitude, even when the team is simply doing its job.
9. **Be a connector:** Break silos and build bridges.
10. **The personal is political:** Learn more about the individual to understand his or her motivations, including fun activities, such as socializing outside the office.

MARÍA GABRIELA "GABY" PACHECO

María Gabriela "Gaby" Pacheco was born on January 28, 1985, in Guayaquil, Ecuador and immigrated to the United States with her parents when she was eight years old. She is a DREAMer with Legal Permanent Residency, and her parents are undocumented. She graduated with with a BS in Special Education K-12, with Specialization in Reading and Second Language Learners from Miami Dade College in 2009. On January 1, 2010, along with three friends, she led the Trail of Dreams, a four-month walk on foot from Miami, Florida to Washington, DC, to call attention to the plight of immigrant families under the threat of deportation. Pacheco is currently the director of advocacy at TheDream.US. In 2012, as political director for United We Dream, she spearheaded the efforts and strategy that led to the approval of the Deferred Action for Childhood Arrivals (DACA) program. Some of the many awards she received include the Mexican American Legal Defense Education Fund Excellence in Community Service Award in 2019, the Adelante Award for Community Leadership in 2018, the Mexican Ohtli Award in 2018, the Americans for

Immigrant Justice Holly Skolnick Human Rights Award in 2017, the Forbes 30 under 30 in Education in 2015, the Forbes 40 Under 40: Latinos in American Politics in 2015 and the YWCA USA Women of Distinction Advocacy and Civic Engagement Award in 2014. On April 22, 2013, Pacheco became the first undocumented Latina to testify before Congress.

⌒⌒ ⌒⌒

Gaby's Top 10 Leadership Lessons

1. **Let love be your guiding light:** With your actions and words, even in the most awful circumstances, act with love.
2. **Learn to say no:** Saying no can mean saying yes to yourself. Be true to your needs and wants, and just say no when it's appropriate.
3. **Leadership = Others:** You can't be a leader of none. Leadership means working with others, learning from others and including others.
4. **What you think expands:** Like a seed that gets planted in your mind, what we think expands and grows in your mind. Be careful with your thoughts, stay positive and believe in the power to accomplish anything you set your mind to. If you think it, it can be done.
5. **Don't run on fumes:** Don't believe the hype; it is neither good nor advantageous for you to overdo things. Over-stressing your body will not only hurt you physically, but it will also make you less effective. If you need to take a break, take it!
6. **Learn to pass the baton:** The greatest leaders are not only mentoring people around them; they also know when to pass on the leadership baton.
7. **Surround yourself with all kinds of people:** Harmony in music is not made by everyone singing the same note; harmony is made by having different people sing different notes simultaneously. It's important to hear and have people of different opinions surrounding you. The world would be pretty flat if it weren't for a diversity of thought.

8. **Bring a chair or build a bigger table:** Always be ready to bring a chair to the table or make the table bigger to allow others in the discussion. Many times, at the decision table, people who should have a voice in the discussion are missing. Learn to spot those holes and be audacious enough to bring others along.
9. **Be fearless:** Fear is a natural reaction of the body to protect yourself from harm. Most fears we have are harmless, so go in with all the certainty of your values and knowledge with everything you do.
10. **It's okay not to know:** Be shrewd and practical. We don't know everything, and that's okay. Leaders are not afraid to ask for help and when to raise their hands to ask questions.

ANN-GEL S. PALERMO

Ann-Gel S. Palermo earned her BS in Biology from SUNY College at Brockport in 1997, her Master of Public Health in Health Management & Policy from the University of Michigan School of Public Health in 1999 and her doctorate in Public Health from the City University of New York Graduate School of Public Health and Health Policy in 2012. Since 1999, she has served as the chief program officer of the Office for Diversity and Inclusion of the Mount Sinai Health System and the associate dean for Diversity and Inclusion in Biomedical Education at the Icahn School of Medicine at Mount Sinai. Palermo co-founded the nonprofit Harlem Community & Academic Partnership, Inc. in 1999, the East Harlem Emergency Preparedness Collaborative in 2013 and, most recently, the East Harlem Community Organizations Active in Disasters. She has received numerous recognitions and awards, including being named to the Top 25 Diversity Leaders in Healthcare by *Modern Healthcare*; she is a fellow of the Aspen Institute Health Innovators, a member of the Aspen Global Leadership Network and a graduate of the National Hispana Leadership Institute Executive Leadership Program.

ᘓᕯ ᕤᕬ

Ann-Gel's Top 10 Leadership Lessons

1. **Develop a healthy and just sense of professional selfishness:** At the end of the day, you are committed to something bigger than yourself, such as social justice and equity. To stay in this commitment, you must develop this mental muscle or mindset that will always ask of you, *What's the yield to me if I pursue [fill in the blank]?* The yield to you can be many things, such as a new network, a new skill set, new knowledge, a specific experience, a new title or role.

2. **Always have a positioning strategy:** The strategy does not have to be fleshed out, but you should always have a sense of tactical maneuvers (positioning) that result in a yield to you. But you have to learn to filter out opportunities or asks of you that have no yield.

3. **Distinguish between the "Mommy's little helper" ask versus the doing a "Shitty little job" (SLJ):** Assess the ask of you and if you cannot distinguish a yield to you (see lesson 1), then it is a "Mommy's little helper" job—only the "Mommy" benefits, and there is no yield to you. Unlike the SLJs, there is a yield, even if it is a small yield that positions you closer to your next tactical maneuver toward that high impact leadership role you envision for yourself. However, you cannot develop this mindset, engage in the positioning strategy and distinguish the yield alone.

4. **Have a coach and be coachable:** A coach is different from a mentor. The coach will hold you accountable for what you said you were going to do by when you said you were going to do it. The coach will always ask the question, "What is the yield to you in doing [XYZ]?" The coach will help you distinguish your non-negotiable guidelines, which help clarify the positioning strategy parameters and keep you focused. The coach is 100% about straight talk, so you have to be coachable.

5. **Learn how to influence without authority:** When we do not have positional power in a system, we must learn to influence the stakeholders who do have positional power. This strategy is linked to fostering shared leadership and accountability.

6. **Always articulate the "shared it."** First be clear on what the "it" is in your mind, and then determine how that "it" can be shared with the other party or how they can buy into the same agenda (your "it"). Getting to the shared "it" also means unpacking what is important to the other party.

7. **Listen carefully to what is being said and what is not being said:** The other party does not always initially share their concerns, needs, ideas or insights. Listen for what is left unsaid and then unpack it.

8. **Learn to ask the wicked questions:** These are the simple questions that address what is left unsaid. These questions disrupt the either/or thinking and consider both/and approach. These questions confront why there has to be only one right way to approach an issue. Asking the wicked questions fosters a critical consciousness within you.

9. **People always remember how you left not when you arrived:** The impact you have on others as a leader will always last longer than the moment you first joined the "team." To be remembered as a strategic thinker and doer with a critical consciousness who can influence without authority and still have impact is what will matter in the long run.

10. **Own your greatness because no one else will and you must remember to acknowledge the greatness in your team members when they cannot do it themselves:** Expect and tune into when your imposter syndrome voice comes up because although it will never go away, you can manage it with various techniques ranging from meditation to leveraging community support structures.

ANNETTE QUIJANO

Annette Quijano was born to Puerto Rican parents on July 4, 1962, in Trenton, New Jersey. She earned her BS in Science in Management from Rutgers University of Camden in 1988 and her JD from Rutgers School of Law in Newark in 1991. Quijano was elected to the New Jersey Assembly in 2008, where she currently is majority conference leader. Since 2009, she also has served as the municipal prosecutor for the City of Elizabeth. Her political career began as a teen advocate organizing a grassroots campaign to dispute a local cable company's decision to eliminate Spanish-language programming. This led to a growing recognition and her election as the youngest board member of the Puerto Rican Congress of New Jersey (PRC). While in the PRC, she became its youngest vice president. Later in her career, Quijano served as assistant governor's counsel for three governors. Quijano has served on the National Hispanic Caucus of State Legislators and was chairperson of the Hispanic Delegation on

Racial Equity, an initiative of the National Conference of State Legislators. Among her most notable awards are the Legislative Award of the New Jersey AFL-CIO (2021), the "Madrina" Award of the Puerto Rican Alliance of Elizabeth (2019), the Celebrating Women's Leadership Honor of the Young Women's Christian Association (2018) and the Legislator of the Year Award of the New Jersey Conference of Mayors (2013).

ഗ⊘ ⊙ᘛ

Annette's Top 10 Leadership Lessons

1. **Know your worth:** There are often people who want to minimize you, diminish your achievements or take advantage of you. Know your worth and your value. Before you can demand respect from others, you first must respect yourself and what you bring to the table.

2. **Network with all kinds of people:** We each have a part to play, from the "lowliest" to the "highest"; each contributes to the final product. Appreciate how every other person, from the janitor to the CEO, contributes to your work environment and accomplishments.

3. **Get a mentor:** In our fast-paced and complex world, it may be difficult to identify a single individual who will assume the role of mentor, guiding you along your professional development. Don't let that stop you. Adapt to the times. Find several persons who can provide the nuggets you need on a given matter rather than putting it all on one person.

4. **Be prepared and be on time:** Don't be one of those who's trying to "wing" it. Do your homework. You are your best salesperson. Your value should be obvious to others by the time and energy you put into being prepared. That shows respect for others' time and effort.

5. **Don't let others define who you are:** Too many of us along the way, especially the "first" in our family, have had our dreams squashed by someone who assumed we were reaching beyond our capabilities. Don't let others' assumptions or stereotypes limit you. The only picture that truly matters is the one you have of yourself. Reach for the stars!

6. **Know where you come from to help you get to where you're going:** My family struggled to make something of themselves. They had it hard. When I get discouraged, I just think of the strong family stock I come from and that pushes me to work at least as hard as they did.

7. **Be a cheerleader for others:** We all need encouragement and reinforcement as we face life's challenges, both personal and professional. Be generous with your recognition. There's plenty to go around. Be supportive and revel in each other's achievements.

8. **Don't sugar coat it:** Be neither an idealist nor a cynic in describing the road ahead. Every road has its ups and downs, and part of deciding which road to take lies in recognizing and accepting the negatives that invariably go along with any professional pursuit.

9. **Share your goals:** Sometimes we don't share our hopes and dreams with others because women are often told that they're too direct or that their ambition is unseemly. But it's okay to say what you want, to express your interest and to go for it. You never know who can help you. But for sure you won't get help if they don't even know what you want.

10. **Know that not everyone is going to be your friend:** Inevitably, you'll get off on the wrong foot with someone or find yourself in competition for the same position. Try your best to get along with everyone and to deal with others with integrity and respect. But don't fret the times when you just can't make a relationship work. It's gonna happen.

MARA CANDELARIA REARDON

Mara Candelaria Reardon was born on July 25, 1965, in East Chicago, Indiana. She received her BA in Liberal Arts from Indiana University Northwest and then attended John Marshall Law School in Chicago, Illinois. She is a former state representative, the first Latina elected to the Indiana General Assembly, in 2006. She was also the first Latina elected as the Indiana House Democratic Caucus chair, in 2018. Currently, Mara is a Partner at MCR Partners, LLC and serves on the Board of Directors of Indiana American Water. Previously, Reardon served as the executive director of the Lake County Drug-Free Alliance. Additionally, she served on the Indiana Commission for Women, Market Development Recycling Board, Minority and Women's Business Enterprise Commission, Hispanic/Latino Affairs Commission and the Indiana Commission to Combat Substance Abuse. Reardon is a co-founder of the National Latina State Legislative Caucus of the Board of Latino Legislative Leaders. Her numerous awards include the Lake County Women's Democratic Club Woman of the Year and the Social Workers' Association Legislator of the Year.

ᥱᏮ ᏮᏅ

Mara's Top 10 Leadership Lessons

1. **Be prepared:** We must always be prepared, whether it is for a meeting or a presentation, speaking engagement or a reception. Know the subject matter, the players, your opposition and your allies.

2. **Respect and value those around you:** Treat all people, not only with professionalism, but also with kindness and respect. We all have a job to do, and we are all dealing with things in our personal life. A warm greeting, a heartfelt compliment or a cup of coffee can really have an impact on your peers and those you work with, whether they are support staff or your bosses. You didn't get to be leader by yourself; recognize those around you as leaders in training.

3. **Don't ask of others what you are not willing to do yourself:** As a leader, you must be willing to roll your sleeves up and dive into tasks that may not be your responsibility. People do not respect a leader who see certain tasks as below them.

4. **Self-care is essential:** To be at our best we need to ensure that we take care of our minds and bodies. Eating right, sleeping well and exercising are very important to your success. Take time for yourself, whether by practicing yoga, meditating or getting a massage. Self-care is essential, because if you don't take care of yourself, you won't be around long enough to take care of others.

5. **Know your worth:** As Latinas, we are great at so many things that don't come naturally for men. Recognizing your worth and negotiating salaries commensurate with your skills and experience is important. Do not settle for less than your worth; it will not help you become a great leader and it will not help those who come after you.

6. **Be on time and stay on schedule:** Being on time shows others that you respect other people's time and staying on schedule keeps you productive.

7. **Learn how to say no:** As leaders, we are often asked to speak at events or make appearances. While it is an honor to be in demand, you cannot physically attend every event. A work-life balance is important.

8. **Meet with and speak to everyone:** Networking has been touted as important to success because it is! Some people collect snow globes; I collect people. It is important not only to your success; it can be an important way to problem-solve and help others. I may not have all the answers, but I'm sure I can connect with someone who does.

9. **Be a person of your word:** If you make commitments to projects, people or tasks, follow through. Leaders need to be reliable and consistent not only for their own success, but for the success of those around them.

10. **Evolve:** The world is ever changing. We must be adaptable to change. Whether its technology that provides us with information in real time or rapid social and political change, leaders must adapt to that change. We can't control everything, but we can control how we react to change.

NEREIDA "NELLIE" RIVERA-O'REILLY

Nellie Rivera-O'Reilly was born on September 8, 1964, in St. Croix, Virgin Islands. She earned a BS in Business Management and Finance at the University of the Virgin Islands and also studied Accounting/Paralegal Studies at the University of Phoenix in Florida in 2008. She is a business co-owner of Sonyas LLC. A certified professional in Human Resources with over fifteen years of experience working as a real estate paralegal, she was elected to the Virgin Islands State Legislature for five terms. She has also served on the Board of the Education Commission of the States, the National Conference of State Legislators Women's Legislative Network, the National Latina State Legislative Caucus of the Board of Latino Legislative Leaders and the National Hispanic Caucus of State Legislators. Rivera-O'Reilly has received numerous recognitions, including Elected Official of the Year of the Virgin Islands National Social Workers Organization (2014) and the Women in Business Speak Off Competition (2004).

 భుర్ ఆరి

Nellie's Top 10 Leadership Lessons

1. **It's okay to show vulnerability:** Your life experiences and adversity may serve to encourage others.
2. **Surround yourself with the best:** Surround yourself with people who truly love you for who you are and who seek nothing from you, as you will be empowered by their love and strength.
3. **Create a safe space:** It is important to have a safe place, "safety net," for yourself and others, where you can find solace and peace when feeling overwhelmed. Here, you will have the ability to put down your armor and just be in your "safe" space.
4. **Be a good steward:** You have a responsibility to honor people's trust and tax dollars, and a responsibility to yourself to keep your promises.
5. **Speak your truth:** Even if it means you will lose friends and make enemies, you will gain peace and preserve your integrity.
6. **Pass the baton:** Recognize and celebrate your impactful work and invite others into the process to learn in an effort to grow more leaders. Know when to step away, avoid burnout and make way for new leaders and new energy.
7. **Seek and accept feedback:** Growth mindset is a key component for leadership. Asking mentors and peers for feedback to see what others see, keeps you grounded. Seek advice.
8. **Listen to what is not said and said:** Sometimes people speak through body language or codes and are very unaware of what is being communicated without speech. Embrace the opportunity to address this.
9. **Trust your skills:** It is imperative to be your authentic self, representing all that you love and are. You are at the table working to not have our community on the menu.

10. **Challenge ideas, create your ideas:** So many times we are in spaces where others in positions of power think they know what is right with wrong ideas. Gracefully show them truth. Be and live your truth.

MARIA ROBLES MEIER

Born in Albuquerque, New Mexico, in 1966 as the seventh generation of a Mexican-American family, Robles Meier studied International Relations at Stanford University. She is the founder and chief strategist of We Are the People, an organization to promote public service and provide leadership development for diverse professionals who impact policy and politics. For a number of years, Robles Meier served as a congressional staffer in senior level positions in both the House of Representatives and the Senate Democratic leadership offices, including senior advisor to the Senate Democratic Leader (2011-2016), executive director for the Congressional Hispanic Caucus (2002-2005) and others dating back to 1999. Also, she was the executive director of the Congressional Hispanic Caucus and led the United States Senate Democratic Diversity Initiative. She has received numerous awards, including being named by the *National Journal* as one of the twenty most powerful staffers on Capitol Hill (2015) and the Certificate of Congressional Service in Recognition of Outstanding Service to Community and Nation (2004).

ⲥⲟ⑤ ⑤ⲟⲩ

Maria's Top 10 Leadership Lessons

1. **Assume you are going to end up somewhere different than where you thought you were headed:** Having a plan is important, but don't let it limit you. Be open to the detours that life puts in your path. It is through the unexpected that we can learn the most.

2. **Stop "shoulding" all over yourself:** You will often encounter others who try to "should" you, because they think they know what is right for you. However, the secret to living an authentic life is listening to your heart. Support others who seek the same opportunity to follow their dreams.

3. **Focus on what you have, not what you don't, and on what you can do, not what you can't:** Beginning with the positive makes it easier to take that first step, and that is the one that really counts.

4. **Express gratitude:** Science has shown that being grateful is good for the brain. Say thank you regularly for things small and large; write thank-you notes and take time to recognize what others have done for you.

5. **Spend your energy on developing your accomplishments, not your titles:** It is fine to want to be recognized for your work, but what you do for others is far more important than the words on a business card.

6. **Make resiliency a goal:** Everyone will face challenges in life; true growth comes through these challenges. With a mindset of resiliency, we focus our energy and efforts on bouncing back, learning and adapting from our setbacks.

7. **Never stop learning:** The process of learning is lifelong. Surround yourself with individuals and situations that can provide you opportunities to grow. Be open to stepping outside your comfort zone to expose yourself to new ideas, people, places and things.

8. **Remember the mind/body/spirit connection:** We are all composed of many interconnected parts. Whether we have a formal belief system or not, we live healthier lives when we expand our minds, nurture our bodies and connect to something outside of ourselves.

9. **Make time and space for creativity in your life:** You don't have to be an artist to embrace creativity. Anything that lets you explore and have fun can trigger your creative process, and this, in turn, makes you a better thinker.

10. **Take public speaking lessons:** No matter what your profession, learning the skills to effectively deliver your message can make you more impactful and help you achieve the results you want.

CARMEN ROSALES

Carmen Rosales has run Kansas' oldest family-owned Mexican restaurant when her parents established the small business in 1963 in Wichita. In addition to being a successful small business owner, Carmen raised five powerful daughters, including two who manage the restaurant and three who are in public service with health foundation, federal law enforcement and state government. Rosales serves as a local matriarch in the community, as well as a role model for runners. She has run over thirteen marathons nationwide and continues to stay active in cycling and pickle ball. She is most active in her Catholic faith through prayer and acts of service and has served as a church lector for years. She is the proud grandmother of five grandchildren.

ഏ ഩ

Carmen's Top 10 Leadership Lessons

1. **Allow God in your life**: God will center you, especially when you most need it. Be open to this and the gifts given to you for service to others.
2. **Take a leap of faith**: Just do it. God will carry you through thick and thin. The will of God will not take you where the grace of God will not protect you.
3. **Love:** You must love yourself in order to love others. Living this example is not easy, but it is worth it.
4. **Hope**: Hope can be your driving and motivating force. It keeps you hungry and focused on your goal. It's good, positive energy.
5. **Discipline:** Identify your goals and eliminate all the nonsense that interferes. Work diligently and keep your goals and stay focused. The harder the goal, the sweeter the victory.
6. **Be grateful:** Thank God all the time. Thank yourself. Thank your initiative, your faith and your freedom. YOU did it. Celebrate your accomplishments and be happy over the moon.
7. **Practice courage:** Do it afraid. Follow your gut and your heart. Fear is not an option. Eliminate and go forward. Be persistent, and never give up.
8. **Stay dedicated:** Get educated. Stay educated. There is no room for complacency. Always look for ways to improve. Failure can be extremely motivating, as it makes you hungry to explore other positive approaches.
9. **Be humble:** Take a deep breath and look back at how much you have overcome and accomplished and thank God for all your hardships and blessings.
10. **Have joy/peace:** After all the hardships and goals and achievements, there is sweet peace, sweet joys and sweet silence to listen to your happy heart.

ANGELIQUE SINA

Angelique Sina was born on September 7, 1988, in Aguadilla, Puerto Rico. She received her BS in Business Administration from the University of Puerto Rico in Aguadilla in 2010 and her Master in Communications Degree from Johns Hopkins University in 2013. Currently, Sina is a global relationship manager at the International Finance Corporation, a member of the World Bank Group. In 2016, she was appointed by the Mayor of Washington, DC, to serve as commissioner for the Latino community. Sina co-founded Amigas and the Latina Impact Fund, which aim to develop female leaders through angel investing. She is also a co-founder and executive director of Friends of Puerto Rico, a national non-profit organization that invests in the orange economy on the island and supports arts and education. She is a trustee of New York Foundling and sits on the boards of the Friends of the Art Museum of the Americas, Latinas in Business, *Viva Latino* magazine, International Finance Corporation's Women's Network and National Society of Hispanic MBAs DC Chapter.

Angelique's Top 10 Leadership Lessons

1. **Don't just wish for it:** Pray for it, plan it and mitigate your risks.
2. **Your net worth is your network:** Actively and strategically meet new people to increase your value.
3. **Negotiate all terms and always, always ask for a discount.**
4. **Always maintain an altruistic attitude:** "We need leaders not in love with money but in love with justice. Not in love with publicity but in love with humanity." –Martin Luther King Jr.
5. **Start investing in your 20's so that you can be in the millions by your mid-thirties.**
6. **Diversification is key:** Diversify your networks, income, hobbies and investments.
7. **Keep your values:** The moment you sacrifice your values, you have failed. A CEO's role is to lead with integrity; the rest can be hired.
8. **Lead with vision:** A leader's vision needs to be strong enough to carry her through to the final goal.
9. **Dream big:** Aspire to goals so big that they scare you when you write them down.
10. **Don't be afraid of failure:** "Winners are not afraid of losing. But losers are. Failure is part of the process of success. People who avoid failure also avoid success." –Robert Kiyosaki

HILDA L. SOLIS

Hilda L. Solis was born on October 20, 1957, in Los Angeles, California to immigrant parents, her mother from Nicaragua and her father from Mexico. She received a BA in Political Science from California State Polytechnic University, in Pomona. She is currently the chair of the Los Angeles County Board of Supervisors, representing more than two million residents of the First District since 2014. After college, Solis became an early advocate for workers' rights, better wages and workplace safety and eventually was appointed Secretary of Labor (2009-2013) by President Barack Obama. Before making history as the first Latina to serve in the presidential cabinet, Solis served in both chambers of the California State Legislature (1992-2009). Solis was the first Latina ever elected to the state senate (1994). In 2000, Solis became the first woman to be awarded the John F. Kennedy Profile in Courage Award.

ᴄᴓ ᴓᴠ

Hilda's Top 10 Leadership Lessons

1. *Tener ganas:* My parents taught me to have *ganas*, that fire in your belly, and it is something that resonates with me each day.
2. **Be kind:** Remember that every act of kindness is also an act of courage. You never know what challenges people are facing at any given time, so your consistent kindness will be there to lift up someone when they are down.
3. **Surround yourself with smart people:** Draw on the creativity and intelligence of your team. Great ideas are not created in a vacuum but are, instead, inspired by teamwork.
4. **Be a sponge:** Seek out knowledge and absorb new information. Hearing different perspectives and learning from others will only add to your development.
5. **Build through community:** Connecting with others and realizing solutions to issues in partnership with community is key.
6. **Be humble:** Recognize there is always something new to learn, even after decades of experience. You should be willing to engage with someone with whom you disagree because you never know when they might be able to teach you something new.
7. **Be steadfast in your values:** Be bold and fight for what you believe. Some things are non-negotiable.
8. **Empower others:** We stand on the shoulders of those who came before us. As Latinas, we must lift each other up and bring others with us along the way. Reach out to those who are just beginning their careers and find ways to support them.
9. *Más juntas, más fuertes*: This is how we lead, by doing so together. Create coalitions that include diverse viewpoints. You'll be stronger for it.
10. **Move forward:** It can be easy to dwell on the past and what could have been done differently. Always continue to look and move forward. Change is incremental.

EVA MARÍA TORRES HERRERA

Eva María Torres Herrera was born on May 31, 1963, in Mexico City, Mexico. In 2006, she immigrated to the United States with her family. In 1987, she graduated with her Business Administration degree from Universidad Autónoma Metropolitana and pursued her graduate studies in Systemic Pedagogy (2005-2006). Torres Herrera has served in the leadership of DREAMers' MOMS since 2013. DREAMers MOMS is the National Movement of Women and Mothers for a just immigration reform, which she helped form in Virginia, Maryland and Washington, DC. She served as the organization's president in 2017 and vice president in 2020. In 2015, Torres Herrera served as the co-founder of Educando con Amor, a community program on education and training for work.

ೞ ര

Eva María's Top 10 Leadership Lessons

1. **Your family is your strength:** Find your internal strength in your family, parents, grandparents and ancestors. Every day I connect internally with my roots. And I remember the words of my mother when I left Mexico: "Never forget where you come from and always help your Latino community."
2. *¡Escucha!* **Listen!:** Listen carefully to what people tell you, look closely around your community, walk through its streets and you will know how you can get involved.
3. **Share your story; it strengthens others:** Telling your story as an immigrant inspires and strengthens others. It is not always easy to tell our story as immigrants. When I first told my story, I realized that it strengthened others and that it strengthened me too.
4. **Learn from leaders around you:** Always admire and respect the people around you. It is an honor to meet new people, since I always learn from them, from their life experiences and from their successes.
5. **Difficult times lead to growth opportunities:** See difficulties as opportunities to gain experience. When I have experienced some difficulty, it leads me to learn, investigate, ask questions and generate resources. And I always say, "Everything has a solution."
6. **Surround yourself with a support network:** Circle yourself with a support network of friends and family. My family and friends are my support network. I listen and reflect on their opinions when I feel under a lot of stress.
7. **Consistency and commitment:** They are two of the tools that I practice daily. When people see consistency and commitment in you, you are a trustworthy person for your community.

8. **Determine to finish:** For me it means, no matter how long it takes me to conduct the projects, they will be carried out.
9. **Always build alliances:** Build alliances with people and organizations. When organizations see your commitment and perseverance, not only are you trustworthy with your community, but also other organizations join you to serve our community together.
10. **Love, passion and faith:** I love and I am passionate about what I am currently doing for my community in education and training for work. Believe that education is power.

HELEN IRIS TORRES

Helen Iris Torres was born on January 17, 1969, in Ponce, Puerto Rico, and raised outside of Detroit, Michigan. She received her BA in Communication in 1991 and her Master in Communications and Urban Studies from Michigan State University in 1991 and 1993, respectively. Torres is the CEO of Hispanas Organized for Political Equality (HOPE), where she leads one of the nation's most influential Latina organizations. HOPE has trained more than 1,200 Latinas for leadership, resulting in over 900 positions. Torres has served as an advisor to projects such as "The Shriver Report: A Woman's Nation Changes Everything," for the Center for American Progress in 2013. Other commissions and boards she has served on include the Alliance for a Better Community (2014-present), the Public Policy Institute of California (2019-present), the Wells Fargo Community Advisory Board (2018-2019), the Southern California Edison Consumer Advisory Board (2015-2018), the *La Opinión* newspaper (2014-2016) and the National Campaign to Prevent Teen and Unplanned Pregnancies (2005-2015). Torres has received numerous awards, including the Giver Award from Hispanics in Philanthropy (2018), the Advocate of the Year by the California Hispanic Chambers of Commerce (2013) and the President's Award of the Millennium Momentum Foundation Inc. (2005).

ೕ ல

Helen's Top 10 Leadership Lessons

1. **Don't idolize your heroes:** No one is perfect; everyone is flawed. Being disappointed by a mentor or a public figure is part of sorting through "why" you followed them in the first place. It helps you define your values.
2. **Respect yourself and others:** Show up ready to lead and listen by respecting others in your group and, just as important, respecting those who don't agree with you. I start out from a place of respect and adjust accordingly. There is never a good reason to be a bully or act in an immature, hurtful way. However, standing up for yourself and your community should never be compromised.
3. **Be purposeful:** If you believe in yourself, make time to invest in your future and the future of your community by having a plan that leads you to your goals. Time is the most precious gift we have; being purposeful ensures you will not waste it.
4. **Take time to heal, but do not wallow in pity:** You will be disappointed, you will have defeats and you will need time off. Step aside, take the time you need, but learn from the situation and get back in the fight. We need every social justice warrior on the front lines.
5. **Prepare to pass the baton:** Life is about the journey. In your journey, build a team that will help you achieve your dreams and advance society. If you are fighting for social justice, remember the fight is never over; there are always others who want to take away your power. Building others up will build our community and move us forward.
6. **Humor is key:** If you can find a way to laugh a little every day, if it is at yourself or the absurdity of a situation or just watching a comedy, treat yourself to a good laugh that will feed your soul.

7. **Be your biggest cheerleader:** Don't wait for the approval of others or acknowledgement. Build your confidence up through self-love. You got this!

8. **Love your family but know when it's time to break away:** As Latinas, family is a core value we all share, but some family members may not share your same world vision. Know when you need to break away in a respectful way and never shy away from an opportunity to educate a family member. Knowing how much energy you want to give away to an individual is an important gage you need to develop. Never give away your power, regardless of who the person is.

9. **Be a lifelong learner:** We all have biases; listening and learning from others helps us be more compassionate leaders. Continuing our formal or informal education will allow us to be part of every generation's teachings.

10. **Don't be a martyr:** Yes, you will have to make sacrifices. Yes, it is not easy to be a leader. But being a leader should bring you joy and purpose.

ANNA TOVAR

Anna Tovar was born on September 25, 1974, in Phoenix, Arizona. She earned her BA in Elementary Education from Arizona State University in 1996 and a real estate license in 2016. She was elected to the Arizona Corporation Commission in 2020 as the first Latina to hold statewide office. Tovar worked as a teacher from 1996 to 2001 and then served on the Tolleson City Council from 2001 to 2009. She served in the Arizona House of Representatives from 2009 to 2012, and in the Arizona Senate from 2012 to 2015. While in the Senate, she served as the senate minority leader and was the Arizona Latino Caucus chair. In 2016, Tovar was elected mayor of Tolleson, Arizona, and is the first woman to hold that office. Among her numerous awards are the Arizona Cities and Town Legislator Champion (2011, 2012, 2013, 2014), the 2013 EMERGE Woman of the Year (2012) and the Hispanic 40 Under 40 Business Leader (2012). She has served on the boards of Jobs for America's Graduates, the Greater Phoenix Economic Council, the Maricopa Association of Governments and the Arizona League of Cities and Towns.

ⁿⁿ ∞

Anna's Top 10 Leadership Lessons

1. **You're stronger than you know:** Sometimes life throws you curve balls, and things may not go as you planned. During these moments, stay strong and determined.
2. **Don't wait to be invited:** Bold decisions require you to be at the table instead of on the menu. Bring your own chair to the table. Always trust your gut instinct.
3. **Stay focused:** Many will try to distract you from your goals. Stay on your path and always have a plan B and C.
4. **Listen, listen, listen:** Everyone has a story that matters. Make it a goal to listen more than you speak. Take what you learn and empower yourself and others.
5. **Get back up:** Never fear change. When you fall, build yourself up stronger than ever.
6. **Collations matter:** Build honest and trustworthy relationships with people and organizations. First, focus on what you have in common and build from there.
7. **Stop worrying:** Don't waste your precious energy on worrying. Switch that worry into positive vibes.
8. **Remember where you came from:** Draw strength from your ancestors. Be proud of who you are and where you came from. Educate, empower and lead.
9. **Be a mentor, ask for a mentor:** Always give back by taking time for our youth. Always ask for a mentor too, as you can always learn something new.
10. **Learn to say no:** Taking care of yourself should be your first priority. Delegating tasks is leadership. Take time for you and the things that make you happy.

LORENA TULE-ROMAIN

Lorena Tule-Romain was born on April 10, 1989, in Michoacán de Ocampo, Mexico, and immigrated to the United States at the age of nine. She was undocumented from 1998-2014 and became a naturalized citizen in 2016. She earned a BA in Government and Spanish Literature from the University of Texas at Austin in 2011 and a Master in Higher Education in 2020 and a doctorate in Higher Education Leadership from Southern Methodist University in 2020. Tule-Romain is the co-founder and chief strategy officer of ImmSchools, an immigrant-led organization that supports undocumented K-12 students and families. Prior to working at ImmSchools, she was a teacher assistant in Bogotá, Colombia. Tule-Romain serves as the Education Coordinator for the North. She received the University of Texas System Bill Archer Fellowship in 2011 and the National Hispana Leadership Institute Latinas Learning to Lead Fellowship in 2010.

ᘒᗱ ᗱᘒ

Lorena's Top 10 Leadership Lessons

1. **Be unapologetic:** Always be proud of your roots and your ancestors because you are their wildest dream. When you show up, do not be afraid to be your unapologetic self.
2. **Dare to dream:** Do not doubt your ability to dream and fight for your dreams to become a reality. Do not let your fear and insecurities hold you back from achieving what your heart desires. Reject any societal expectations and create your own destiny.
3. **Listen to your heart:** When we are truly honest with ourselves, we can see our true potential. Take time to listen to your inner voice and embrace what you have to offer.
4. **Build a community:** Surround yourself with a diverse set of individuals who can uplift you and support you throughout your life. Get involved in your community and local politics because it matters what you do.
5. **Embrace change:** Find ways to challenge yourself and your daily routine. Try new foods, see new places, read new books, make new friends.
6. **Love:** Love is an act of resistance and finding ways to love yourself is liberating.
7. **Mental health:** Find time to take care of your wellbeing, schedule meditation, therapy, outdoor walks, talk to a friend, write, etc.
8. **Be a co-conspirator:** Our liberation is bound together, and we must always align with those directly impacted. We must always fight systems of oppression and white supremacy, knowing that the works start with ourselves.
9. **Share your light:** When embarking in a new career or learning something new, share your knowledge with others and open doors for those behind you. You cannot be what you cannot see. We must be role models for our community.
10. **Find joy:** Life can be short. We must find and create joyful memories with those around us.

LETICIA VAN DE PUTTE

Leticia Van de Putte graduated from the University of Texas College of Pharmacy in 1979; in 1994, she was a Kellogg fellow at Harvard University's John F. Kennedy School of Government. While working as a pharmacist, she served in the Texas Legislature for over two decades, beginning in 1980. In 2016, Van de Putte and former Texas Secretary of State Hope Andrade formed Andrade-Van de Putte & Associates, a full-service consulting firm. Nationally, Leticia has served in numerous leadership positions, including with the Mexican American Legal and Defense Educational Fund, the League of United Latin American Citizens and the Latino Leaders Network. She has received more than two hundred awards and citations for her work on behalf of small businesses, veterans, families, quality education, healthcare and economic development. Among these are the Community Advocate of the Year Award (2014), the MALDEF Lifetime Achievement Award (2010), the Edward R. Roybal Award of the National Association of Latino Elected and Appointed Officials (2008),

the Annie's List Woman Warrior Lifetime Achievement Award
(2011) and the National Council of State Legislators Foundation
Outstanding Service and Leadership Award (2014). Van de Putte
is the subject of a book, *Latina Legislator: Leticia Van de Putte
and the Road to Leadership* by Sharon Navarro.

ᥬᥬ ᥬᥬ

Leticia's Top 10 Leadership Lessons

1. **Articulate the greater good:** The purpose of leadership is not personal gain but public good to improve the lives of those in your organization, your neighborhood, your community, your state and nation. It's about the people, not you. Lead with your heart for them.

2. **Be grounded in purpose:** Know why you want to lead, why you ask others to join you in action, then you can work for the best outcome. Your voice, your time, your talent and every action should be done with purpose for a positive outcome.

3. **Be where your feet are:** Some might call this mindfulness. Treat each encounter with the time and respect dignifying the other person or group you are with now instead of looking over their shoulders to see who more important has walked into the room. Concentrate on what's at hand. If you're with family, concentrate on love; if you're at work, concentrate on getting the job done!

4. **Know your sh*t:** Get intelligence, be well versed on your subject matter. Latinas are almost always stereotyped in the media in less than intellectual jobs. Less is more when you speak; know the facts.

5. **Be on time:** The best leaders are respectful of the one commodity you can't regain; lost time equals lost productivity. Be there early, and that's on time. If you're on time . . . your late.

6. **Learn from failure:** Don't expect to be perfect at everything. Things beyond your control can destroy the best planning. Failure is not the outcome; true failure is not learning from your mistakes.

7. **Recognize the potential in those around you and nurture their desire to advance:** Some of the most capable women I've known just needed a little encouragement and guidance. Go beyond being just a mentor; be a connector, an advancer and an advocate for other Latinas. When they shine, your sense of purpose will be validated. Believe me: it's a greatly rewarding and proud moment to see their accomplishments.

8. **Expect betrayal:** The hardest lesson is the loss of trust and credibility from someone or an organization you believed in. Get over it. Every moment spent on despair, revenge and unhappiness is a moment you lose to make the greater good. My motto: there is a fine line between love and hate because there is still a relationship. The opposite of love is, "I don't give you space."

9. **Look at this every day:** MAKE a plan. WRITE that sh*t down. And WORK on it . . . EVERY fu**ing day!

10. **Work hard, pray hard:** You will feel overwhelmed at times. It's like being on a high ladder: Breathe and just don't look down. Stay centered on your purpose, your own worth. Always return to what grounds you: faith. And give thanks to our Creator.

LUZ URBÁEZ WEINBERG

Luz Urbáez Weinberg was born on September 10, 1972, in San Juan, Puerto Rico. She is a graduate in Psychology of Florida International University (2002). She is the CEO of GlobComm, LLC, a communications consulting firm specializing in construction impact mitigation. She served as a commissioner for the City of Aventura, Florida from 2005-2014 and again in 2018. Former Florida Governor Rick Scott appointed Commissioner Weinberg to two 4-year terms on the Miami-Dade Expressway Authority. Her versatile career path has included the position of public relations director and CEO stints in the healthcare and construction industries, including as director of communications for the Port of Miami Tunnel and Brickell City Centre. She has published more than 400 marketing/PR and op-ed articles, as well as a book, *The Port Miami Tunnel Project* (2015). Her most notable awards include the Latina of Influence of *Hispanic Lifestyle Magazine* (2014); the Elected Official of the Year Award from the South Florida Hispanic Chamber of Commerce (2012) and the Pace Setter of the Year Award of the National Conference on Puerto Rican Women (2010).

∽◌ ◌∾

Luz's Top 10 Leadership Lessons

1. **Prior preparation does prevent poor performance:** This is certain in business and politics. Never assume "you got this," even when the task is your "jam." I have always prepared and taken pride in preparing, even for the most mundane of tasks. Preparing shows respect for the work and further engenders confidence in your ability to do it.

2. **Eye contact:** Maintain eye contact in every setting, especially in contentious or even intimidating settings. Eye contact is a sign of respect to your audience and confidence in yourself. Do not break it, and never break it first. It's not a staring contest, though; so, gauge it and be adult about it.

3. **Know your audience and speak their language**: In public speaking, or day-to-day one-on-one, always know your audience and speak to them in terms they will understand. Watch for feedback and adjust accordingly, i.e. read the body, whether it's a group of executives at a board meeting, constituents in a political gathering or your child's sixth-grade career day!

4. **Tell the truth, tell it first, tell it all:** When it comes to crisis management—we all get a crisis or two in our careers—it is always best to "get ahead" of a problem. It is the only way to control the narrative. So, own the mistake, oversight or situation—whatever the case—and get in front of those demanding answers and tell the truth as you know it, tell it first before others distort it and tell it all until they understand. This is a display of good leadership and self-confidence that strengthens your credibility.

5. **Solve a problem:** If you want to be memorable, solve a problem for anyone, a board, a neighborhood group, an ally, an adversary . . . anyone, but solve it. Truly listening to someone's problem and finding a way to resolve it is a sure way to earn their trust and make yourself memorable.

6. **Be clear and precise:** I raised my kids saying, "E-N-U-N-C-I-A-T-E," since they began talking, and they still say that today. If you want to be not just heard, but understood, you must enunciate every word. Practice your speaking! Precise speech is also a sign of knowledge and self-confidence, and that, of course, earns you credibility.

7. **Eliminate clutter and qualifiers:** To be clear and precise, you must speak without clutter or "qualifiers." Think of that teenager in the 1980s who needed reassurance from her audience and always asked, "You know?" or added, "It's like. . . ." Clutter and qualifiers add nothing to your narrative and diminish your credibility. Catch yourself overusing adjectives, too! With clutters and qualifiers on the low, your confidence and credibility goes quite high.

8. **Always have a question:** If you are in a room, any setting of any type, any time, and someone says, "Does anyone have a question?" Always have one, stand up, state your name, your title, your company, and then state whatever question you can drum up. It is never about the question. It's about the freest form of advertising: an open platform for group networking. Please don't be "Heather" from the '80s; state your name, first and last.

9. **Use first and last names:** Even when I am in a non-political, non-business social gathering, I am never "Luz." I am always "Luz Weinberg." I shake hands firmly, look people square in the eyes and enunciate my full name. You never know who you are meeting, and that first impression is what they will remember: an adult with a memorable full name, strong eye-contact and a confident handshake.

10. **Ask for their first and last names:** After being introduced to someone, ask for their full name if they did not give it. If they did, repeat it out loud. Repetition commits things to memory, so you can better remember the name that goes with that face later. Then, during your conversation, say their first name often. In psychology, we say, "Because the ego is so strong, there is no sweeter sound than the sound of your own name." Hearing you say their name a few times will also commit you to their memory and have them think of you as the most awesome person ever. Who are we kidding: you too have an ego, so of course you are!

EPILOGUE

We have read 50 leadership lessons but none of them acted alone. Let us now examine the top ten most common lessons in order of mention by this group. This is not to say other lessons are less important; however, these particular lessons seem to be the most important ones for this group of leaders. In general, we Latina leaders do not operate as individual autocrats; rather we operate from unity, family and a resiliency stemming from our ancestors' strengths. We value the strength in community. What this means for the United States is that the country is benefitting from leaders like us. This is important because our world needs us now and in the future. We now have an amazing opportunity to share with the world another aspect of women's leadership. We have not been waiting for this moment, because we have been preparing ourselves for a long time.

CᕦᎧ Ꭷᕲᕲ

Top Ten Most Common Lessons

1. **Believe in yourself:** We acknowledge that self-confidence can be a challenge, and at the same time, we note our ability to harness our own potential. Our society has influenced us to second guess our unique skills, even though studies show that women are effective communicators, listeners, negotiators and ultimately effective problem solvers. Our Latina leaders note the importance of changing this mindset for our sisters and daughters who will come after us. Believing in ourselves, and each other, will allow us to move mountains. Persistence and taking risks are in our blood. Our potential is powerful, if we let it be powerful. We can think big and dream boldly, so when we write it down and say it out loudly, we tremble. We will work hard on that dream every single day, and we must remind ourselves to trust our authentic selves because we know we are representing all that we love. We work hard to be at the table, so our loved ones are not on the menu. We must practice courage and follow our guts because fear is not an option. Yes, life will get overwhelming, but we will remember to breathe and stay focused on our purpose and self-worth. We can be what we believe, and possibly inspire another person when they see us as an example.

2. **Self-care:** We emphasize the importance of loving ourselves, so we can love others. That means making time to take care of our own health and the things that make us happy. A fun mechanism could involve posting pictures of these things as daily reminders. When we do this, we will be in the best version of ourselves to take care of others in the best way possible for the multiple years we are alive. We highlight the importance of taking time for self-care, whether through mediation, exercise, massage or simply ten minutes alone in our bathrooms. We shall have fun finding creative ways to decompress and recharge.

3. **Be a mentor and a mentee:** This goes back to the notion of surrounding ourselves with people who inspire us, motivate us and hold us accountable. We have learned that we must help others grow and succeed, because others did that for us. We remember when we were the mentee and how helpful it was to have a mentor guide us through land mines and advise us. Because that was such a positive experience for us, we also note the importance of paying it forward by serving as a mentor when we can. Leading by this example continues to advance our world in the process.

4. **Listen:** We stress the importance of serving as an active listener, in listening carefully before we speak. We acknowledge that true leadership requires compassionate listening and watching for non-verbal cues. The bottom line is to listen more than we speak. When we listen, we grow stronger as leaders both personally and professionally.

5. **Be a lifelong learner and embrace change:** We honor our roots and ancestors who have sacrificed for us to be where we are today. We want to use their strength and the lessons learned from their experiences. We are blessed with this time on Earth, where every day is an opportunity to learn and grow to transform into phenomenal humans, a part of something bigger than life itself. Enjoying the learning and change process is crucial. We have learned to challenge ourselves to try new things, whether informally or formally. The challenge can be somewhat formal by taking a class, a personal development program, an executive course, a leadership development program, which can serve as additional credentials or be just for fun. We know it is also important to try new hobbies, food, careers and travels to broaden our horizons and taste buds. If we are not learning in various aspects of our life, then that is a clear sign to change up that area.

6. **Surround yourself with smart people and network:** We value the networks we surround ourselves with, both professional and personal. Our Latina leaders share the empowerment from both circles. For the personal aspect, we find it essential to have our soul sisters around us with whom we can vent, cry, lean on and celebrate openly. For the professional lives, it is imperative to surround ourselves with good, smart people. Sometimes this means going to activities or events to find some of those amazing individuals. Either way, we must be intentional about who we spend our time and life journeys with. These loyal circles of individuals are like our chosen family; they are our protectors and cheerleaders who will keep us accountable and grounded, along with holding space for us to be ourselves. These tribes will support us because they love us unconditionally.

7. **Be a cheerleader, grow other leaders:** We all need encouragement and friendly reminders about how amazing each of us are. When we recognize greatness, we share our loving support for each other's accomplishments. It is our duty to empower each other, especially in celebrating our special successes.

8. **Learn from our failures, pick ourselves up:** We have heard many times the saying "things happen for a reason," and it is tough to take in when we are in the middle of it. We acknowledge that sometimes unexpected situations push us to arrive at our special destination. We have the choice to pay attention to the signs or ignore the signs and continue the longer journey to happiness. We recognize we must embrace our failures and learn the lessons given to us to help us grow. It is not the fall, but it is the way we come back better and improved. We must understand that failure is a part of the road to success, so let us lean in and not allow any missed opportunities to pass us by. Leadership requires taking bold action and working hard with a sense of urgency.

9. **Gratitude:** Gratitude is contagious and inspiring. Whether it is a small act of kindness or a simple thank-you note, acts of gratitude have immediate impact. When we give grace and gratitude, we end up also being the receivers of unexpected gifts and opportunities. We realize we must take time to inhale and exhale as we look back at what we have overcome and accomplished in our lives. For this, we must give thanks to our Creator or whatever higher being we believe in.

10. **Ask for help:** Latina leaders admit we can be better at knowing our limitations and more open to asking for help. Asking for help is an act of self-love. We know it is beneficial to ourselves to be bold and ask people in authority, influencers for support in whatever manner we may need. We all must remind ourselves that there is no one that knows everything, and therefore it is practical to ask for help.

AFTERWORD: MY JOURNEY

I wanted this book to be a gift for readers, and in fact it also ended up being a gift for me as well. I learned so much about my friends and myself in this book. I could hear their voices speaking as I was reading out loud their leadership lessons. I have had the distinct honor and privilege of meeting, working and living around amazing women throughout my life, whether in Kansas, Texas or Washington, DC. I consider myself the luckiest lady in the world to witness and be a part of these amazing women's lives. In connection to these fifty phenomenal women in leadership, I will share parts of my own journey and my own leadership lessons. Hopefully my readers can combine these lessons with their own journeys.

From the moment I was born in 1977, I was exposed to strong Latina leadership. I was raised by my mother Carmen Rosales and three grandmothers: Luisa García, Concepción López and Socorro Tienda. In addition, I had four sisters, Monique, Sonia, Carmen and Adele; tons of aunts and cousins; my *comadres* Carla Bañuelos and Aude Negrete-Baños; and a large extended family of Latinas. I have two cousins who were elected officials in Texas: Texas State Representative Diana Maldonado and Marina García, a constable in Lubbock. My architect, union-leader father James P. García was the eldest of five and came from a servant leadership family in Garden City, Kansas, where my Aunt Irene García was elected one of the first Latinas to the Garden City school board in 1985; and my cousin Elsa Ulrich served as Finney County Clerk from 2005 to 2017.

My sisters and I have always recognized the remarkable opportunities we were given, thanks to the strength and resilience of our families, including our mom's parents, Rafael and Connie López, who adopted her, and our mom's birth parents, Socorro Tienda and José Angel Gaytán, as well as our dad's parents, Luisa and Phillip García. Each set of our grandparents had doctorates in life but some were unable to finish formal high school because they were cleaning people's homes and feeding America as migrant farmworkers picking tomatoes, beets, prunes and more as they followed the seasonal crops across the United States. Our grandfathers Philip and Rafael embraced the United States for the opportunities they were given and bravely served in World War II. My family has always emphasized the importance of hard work, public service and to truly pay it forward to help others.

Also, during World War II, my grandma Luisa's only sister, Katherine Ayala, known to us as Aunt Kate, served as a local leader in the sense that she put on a bandana, like Rosie the Riveter, and went to work with a small group of women at the local air base in the Garden City area when workers were needed. In the 1960s, our grandma Luisa worked in public health at the Sedgwick County Health Department and helped translate for Spanish-speaking families who came to the health department for various reasons. Grandma Connie and grandpa Rafael worked hard to establish small businesses after our grandpa Rafael returned to Wichita, Kansas, from WWII. He opened up a barber shop next to McConnell Air Force Base, and our grandma Connie opened up Connie's Mexico Café in 1963, which today is Kansas' oldest family-owned Mexican restaurant. Fast forward to 1976, when Jimmy Carter was running for president, our family was fortunate that he came to Connie's for a campaign stop. My mom was pregnant with me at the time, and we have all joked that it was then in utero that my love for public service and serving others was formed! My dad's younger brother, Ernie García—Uncle Ernie to us—became the first Latino US Senate sergeant-at-arms, having been nominated by Senator Bob Dole and confirmed by the Senate in 1985. Earlier in our family history, in April 1973, our uncle Dionisio Campos García (brother to our grandpa Philip) was elected mayor of Garden City, Kansas, and his wife, our aunt Irene García, was elected to the board of education in Garden City.

My mother was born in South Texas on the border and was separated from her biological family when she was four years old but reunited with them when she was pregnant with me. This family story is another book in itself; it definitely impacted the way I lived my life. My father is from western Kansas. I consider both Kansas and Texas my home states, as I have lived in both states. My sisters and I were raised in our family restaurant, where customer service was a part of our daily lives. I am the middle of five daughters, and my sisters are fierce women leaders. All five of us García sisters have witnessed powerful servant leadership, beginning when we were kids. All five of us were Girl Scouts and continued growing our leadership skills when we were active members of the Hispanic American Leadership Organization and when we attended college—I was a MEChA member at the University of Texas at San Antonio. Public service and servant leadership has always been a part of our family tradition. We know it is our responsibility to keep growing and to grow the leadership all around us. It has been the strength, resilience and grit of our family that has showed us that we can make a meaningful difference with hard work and love of our country.

Now it's my turn.

DELIA GARCÍA

I was born in in Wichita, Kansas, in 1977. I received my BA in Ethnic Studies and Political Science from Wichita State University in 2002. I went on and received my Masters in Political Science from St. Mary's University at San Antonio, Texas, in 2004. I had additional training at the Harvard University Executive Leadership Program in 2007, the Aspen Institute Executive Leadership Program in 2018 and the Diversity, Equity, Inclusion Certification by the University of Southern Florida. I currently serve as an Equity and Access Expert at the US Department of Labor in Washington, DC. In 2004, I was the first Latina and youngest female elected to the State of Kansas Legislature. In 2019, I was appointed the first Latina secretary of labor in Kansas. In Washington, DC, I served as a CEO and led two national non-profits: ReflectUS, which works to increase women's representation in elected and appointed leadership, and the National Migrant Seasonal Head Start Association, which works with migrant farm worker families. I also worked at the National Education Association as senior liaison to the Latino community. Some of the awards I am proud to have received are the League of Women Voters Centennial Kansas Trailblazers (2020), the Women's Foundation Changemaker Profile Award (2019), the NALFO National Civic Leader Award (2011), the National Latina Trailblazer in Government from the US Hispanic and Latina Chamber of Commerce (2009) and the Mexican American Legal Defense and Education Fund Matt Garcia Public Service Award (2009). My work has been covered by the NBC Nightly News, the Daily Show, the Wall Street Journal, and published in *Newsweek*, *Latina Style* and the *McNair Scholar Program Journal of Research*.

⁎⁎ ⁎⁎

Delia's 10 Leadership Lessons

1. **Be *chingona*:** Take risks. Learn to be comfortable with the uncomfortable and embrace change. At times, I have spoken up with a shaky voice, and it feels really good later.
2. **Find a mentor, be a mentor:** Build a mentor circle of five, and you mentor a circle of five. I make sure my circle is made up of people who I want to be like or experts in my interests.
3. **Be a good listener:** When you listen, people feel valued. When people feel valued, they have ownership in your cause and are motivated to act. Look for and listen to people's strengths and build upon them. You may learn something too.
4. **Believe in yourself:** Start with the idea that you can make things happen before you start talking yourself out of it. Trust your capability to get it done and know you are enough.
5. **Network, network, network:** Build relationships with people you want to be like and with people you want to serve. Powerful networks translate to powerful communities.
6. **Be resilient:** Be tough every time you fail, because when you experience these tests, they make you stronger and wiser. I write an affirmation on a sticky note for me to see daily.
7. **Build a shared vision:** First we listen. Then we talk. Figure it out. Then we agree to act.
8. **Dream big instead of worrying big:** Be an optimist. Have faith in yourself and others. There is really no time for negativity. Don't fall victim to imposter syndrome, which is the idea that you're faking it or that you are not good enough. The world needs our leadership.
9. **Lead with gratitude:** Be grateful for the opportunity to work with others, serve others and serve a cause greater than yourself. I draw strength from my ancestors.
10. **Love yourself:** Make the time to take care of your health, family and social life. Invest in the things that make you happy. I put pictures of this on my vision board to see daily.